A Journal of the Living the One Light Series

SACRED COSMIC

RHYTHMS

2020 JOURNAL

A JOURNAL TO SUPPORT YOUR
SOUL IN THE SACRED WAVES OF 2020

MARTHA ALTER HINES

ISBN: 9781677945269

First printing edition 2019

Also by Martha Alter Hines:
Living the One Light
Gaia Speaks
Cosmos Speaks

www.LivingTheOneLight.com
For more information and bulk orders, please contact:
livingtheonelight@gmail.com

TABLE OF CONTENTS

DEDICATION

I would like to dedicate this journal to YOU and to all of us as a collective.

The year of 2020 holds many possibilties for massive change and massive re-envisioning of ourselves and our world. I am feeling called to assist us all to feel held, to feel seen, to feel deeply valued and needed and to open ourselves up to EVERY SINGLE possiblity in existence of the new ways we can construct our world, construct our ways of being within ourselves, between ourselves, and with our world at large.

I dedicate this journal to the intention and prayer that we, as a collective, will choose in each moment to navigate this year of 2020 with as much self awareness, self love, and dedication to the true love of all of existence and each other as possible. I hope and pray that we move through this year and come out stronger, with a more clear vision and plan for how we are going to individually and collectively live in our world so that we are each treated with respect, love, and care that we each need and deserve and that our entire planet needs and deserves.

So much love...

Martha

INTRODUCTION

Hello, Friends

    I want to start with an introduction in my own voice before I move on to the full channeled message that follows.
I am so happy you are here and using this 2020 Journal!

    My hope with this journal is that it will help to support you and all of us to approach 2020 with a sense of context, direction, and hope for our year and for moving into this next phase of human existence.

    Many of us are looking around at the world and at our planet and feeling an understandable sense of despair, dread, hopelessness, depression, and a sense that the world is on fire, is on the verge of destruction, and so forth. There is SO much trauma and destruction happening on the planet and I see and feel it deeply.

    At the same time, I feel strongly that we are on the planet at this time not to despair, but to pick ourselves up and do what it is we came to do. If we are in a war zone, I do not think we are here to just lay down and die due to the horrific things surrounding us. I think we are here to help pick up the pieces, to be the medics, to be the visionaries and the builders of the new way, whatever we choose for that to be and in the exact ways we, in particing that 2020 could bring a lot of difficulty on many levels. I see that too and I certainly see it when I look around our world. However, what I also see and feel is that these energies and these times give us an opportunity to consciously "get behind" the destruction of the aspects of our current way of doing things on the planet, such as the negative constructs of patriarchy and so forth. As we consciously watch and feel these aspects of ourselves and our world get hit hard with an energy that has the potential to "destroy" a lot of things, we then have the opportunity to simultaneously and collectively envision what we actually WANT in the new era we are moving into. During this year, I also feel that we have a chance to practice, to try out some parts of that new vision we hold through the year. Then as the energies finally move into potentially "lighter" energy on December 21, 2020, we will have the chance to "launch" our practiced visions. I feel strongly that this new vision and new way must be envisioned and practiced on an individual level, within one on one intimate relationships, in groups, and as an entire collective.

So my prayer with this journal is that it will give you an opportunity to connect deeply to your particular, pure truth, the wisdom that needs to come through YOU specifically, the puzzle piece of the vision that we can only get through YOU. I also hope that the journal will provide some insight and context for you in understanding the overarching energies of this year so that you can flow with, rather than fight against, those energies. Ultimately, the energies do have an ability to help us to move into a time that is more expanded, open, supportive, deeply loving, and valuing of each of us and of all life forms. How wonderful is that? We could choose to be on the verge of wonderful things! This is why we are here, right here and right now. Let's do it...

Before we start, I also want to give a couple of overarching caveats or disclaimers as you venture into this journal and this year. First, astrology talks about energies. It talks about potentialities. Some versions of astrology can be predictive and/or fatalistic (in other words, might tell you what WILL happen or give a narrative for you). However, everything is simply energy, including the energies in our bodies, in our spirit selves, and in all of existence, including the energies of this beautiful, amazing solar system that is reflected in astrology. While there is a "narrative" or story being told in this journal about how the energies of the year could be expressed, this is only ONE story. Anything and everything that is expressed through this journal is fully channeled and so I trust it on a particular level. At the same time, it is very much speaking to only ONE level of possibilites that may or may not come to fruition in your life and in our world. The MOST important thing to me is that this journal provide you with an opportunity to check in with your own soul wisdom and to bring that through as much as possible throughout this entire year and moving into the whole next phase of your life. Therefore, if any of the messages or journal prompts simply do not resonate for you or describe a reality that is not yours, just ignore them! Or use them as fodder for thought or discussion. Or just check in with your own soul reality and your own wisdom and take the journaling time to simply be in the flow of YOU. Your reality is the most beautiful thing in existence and is exactly what we all need, right here and right now. So please, above all else, let that shine... that is my prayer for you and for us all.

In addition, I want to note that all astrological phenomena affect each of us differently, just like anything else! In particular, where each event falls in your chart or how it plays into the energies of your natal chart will make a big impact in the ways in which these energies might play out in your life, among many other factors. Feel free to be in touch if you would like to learn more about how these energies may affect you.

I would love to hear your experiences as you journey through the year and am available to help to support you on a personal and group level. I will be offering free videos, as well as paid memberships, workshops, and individual sessions. Please feel free to connect with me at www.livingtheonelight.com or livingtheonelight@gmail.com any time.

So much love,

Martha

WELCOME

Hello and Welcome, Good Friends...

Welcome to the Living the One Light Sacred Cosmic Rhythms Journal for 2020!

We come to you as beings of light who are manifestations of your highest selves in the midst of all of existence.

We come to help to guide you through this next phase of your life on Earth in this wave of energy that you call the year 2020.

We want to give an overview and introduction to this journal and a sense of why we are coming to you with this gift.

THE OVERARCHING ENERGIES OF 2020

As we have said many times before in other places, in the ultimate reality of existence, there is no such thing as time or space. However, in the world that has been constructed by the energies in your realm of things, there is a space and time continuum and you are entering a certain nano-fraction of a second that you are portioning off as "the year 2020." While this concept is a stretch for us to conceptualize or to go along with, we recognize that it is an important construct for you and in your experience of your growth and evolution and in your remembering of all of who you are, both as individuals and as a collective.

Therefore, we will follow this train of thought and give you some insight into what might be coming, energetically, and what may be helpful for you as you move through what you conceive of as this "year."

As you probably know, all of existence is essentially energy. All things are energy. And energy is constantly in motion. Energy is constantly moving and constantly changing. So when we look at the big picture of all of existence, what we see is simply moving energy. And so anything and everything that is happening in your life or on your planet or in your galaxy or anywhere for that matter is simply moving energy.

What we can see is that the energies of the collective, not only in your universe and your solar system, but in existence in general, is that energies are shifting so that there is a "righting" of a balance of things so that all dimensions and all realities are in equal measure with each other. The balance of things has been tilted so that, for example, in your world, the teeter totter or seesaw of energies has been tilted toward you experiencing things in what you consider a "three dimensional, five senses, physical reality" type of experience of things. The teeter totter of energies in all of existence is shifting so that the energies of all things is opening up and the spaces of all things is coming to have more breathing room in a sense. Therefore, one effect of this is that the spaces between all dimensions is opening up and it is becoming much more possible for us all to simultaneously co-exist again as one and for us to get back into a conscious relationship with the all that is.

The rebalancing of this teeter totter of energies in all of existence means many things in your world. Imagine that your world has been on the "down" end of the teeter totter for centuries. So it is as though the weight of most things has been weighing down your world and this weight has made your world feel very dense. As the teeter totter of the energy of existence moves and shifts back up, the weight of things on your end of the teeter totter is going to lessen and loosen and lighten. And as this happens, there will be a major shift in consciousness that has not existed on your planet in eons.

This shift is already happening and has been happening for a while. It will continue to happen.

However, in your exact timeframe of moving from 2019 to 2020 and then into 2021, this shift of the density of things can be seen and reflected in the astrology of your times.

In general, the shift that your consciousness is moving through is from one of density and concrete thinking to an opportunity for openness, lightness, innovation that is light years ahead of what you might imagine, a sense of being in a collective experience, full egalitarianism, and a sense that all beings matter equally, and a reality and way of being of co-creating with all that is. We will describe this more in a bit.

With regard to the energies of 2020, what your astrologers are saying and noticing that in the year 2020, the deep and karmic planets of Pluto and Saturn, as well as the south node of the moon (also representing the past) are all in Capricorn (the sign of the dense, patriarchal past and structure of your societies). And starting on December 2, 2019, but then most significantly starting in January 2020, Jupiter also enters and then moves through the sign of Capricorn, highlighting, hitting, and augmenting the deep, karma dredging effects of Pluto, Saturn, and the south node of the moon all in Capricorn.

Furthermore, Jupiter will be hitting Pluto and Saturn, then going retrograde, and then coming back and hitting those planets again and again in the year of 2020. The purpose of this potentially difficult set of energies is actually a good one. It is actually a great one. It is as though you all have been sitting on that falling end of the seesaw with the density of a patriarchal society that has had so much suffering and so much karmic difficulty and as the seesaw lifts and starts to move, the planets of Pluto and Saturn, as well as the south node of the moon are giving the collective a chance to clear out all of the difficulty of that density that has been sitting on that low end of the seesaw for decades, for centuries, for eons. And then Jupiter will be coming through and assisting those planets in their efforts to dredge up the sludge and clean out that karmic past of all of these eons of the dense existence. And as Jupiter comes through and then goes retrograde and then comes through again, it will clean and clear over and over and over again and it will allow and give your whole collective, as well as you, individually, an opportunity to let go and let go and let go so that you can open back up and clear and breathe again.

And then, by the end of 2020, in December of 2020, Jupiter and Saturn will finally go out of Capricorn and will be conjunct at 0 degrees of Aquarius - an air sign!! And this will bring in air! And the density will lighten for real and the more clearing and cleansing you have done through this time of dredging up things in 2020, you will finally be able to breathe!! And as a collective, hopefully you all will have consciously gone through the collective clearing and the world will hopefully be able to breathe a bit better.

In addition, as Jupiter moves through the planets in Capricorn, then retrogrades, and then hits them again, this is a time of us being able to reflect, revisit, and reflect again, open up to a bigger world, a bigger sense of the possibilities, of what we truly believe and value, and how we want to structure our world and our society. Jupiter brings expansiveness to our sense of structures, our sense of what we value in our societies, and the energy of Capricorn can bring us the energy to put these ideas into concrete manifestation.

So during this time, we invite you to use these energies to immediately begin to reflect, to open up, to get in touch with the truest and highest reality that is you and to both collectively and individually begin to explore what you want this open, more free, more loving and inclusive version of your society to look like. We invite you to use the energies of this year to both dive deep inside yourself for your deepest truths and then also to connect and join together as feels right and true for you to hear, to share, to begin to construct, to tear down, to let fall away, and to re-envision and reconstruct aspects of your world, your economy, your ways of working and being in the world that are of exactly what you hold to be most true and most right here and now. This is the time for doing that. The year 2020 is a time of reflecting, diving deep, coming back up, diving down again, reflecting as a collective, clearing out, letting things fall away, and then putting back the puzzle pieces in ways that truly fit who you are and who you want to be.

So... that brings us to the question we want to address of "How Can I Navigate the Potential Intensities of 2020 In the Best Way Possible?" This is a great question and part of why we have created this journal for you.

Here are some of our thoughts and suggestions. Some of these will resonate more for some of you at certain times and others at other times. Notice what resonates and what doesn't and just try out what works and then try out others and come up with your own. Share what is working for you and help each other out. This is a time of coming together and of working hard together to dig your way out of a dark, difficult time.

SUGGESTIONS FOR NAVIGATING 2020 (and life)

1). Take a deep breath. Literally. Just breathe a LOT. Throughout this time of dredging up karmic difficulties of the collective past of all of existence, it is vital to bring breath and lightness into and through your body. Do this literally by remembering your breath and simply breathe deeply and fully.

2). Ride the waves. At various points in your life and/or in the experience of the collective and of your groups or nations or world, there will be times when it feels like a wave hits. For example, as Jupiter goes retrograde and then goes direct again and hits certain points in the Capricorn degrees, you and the world might have a sense of a mac truck hitting the collective or your own psyche or your own life and as though this mac truck is adding to the dredging of things on various levels. (Jupiter moving through your chart may also have wonderful feeling effects too!). However, if and when it does seem as though a wave or tsunami is hitting in some way, it is great if you are able to catch that wave at the very beginning. In fact, just simply having the perspective that such waves are and will be coming throughout life, but in particular in this year, you will be able to be "ahead of the wave" and will be able to ride on top of it, hopefully rather than getting a sense of being drowned by it. You can do this by simply taking those deep breaths we talked about and by staying aware and mindful of the bigger picture of existence, of the bigger picture of the context of what is happening and the context that the purpose of this experience is ultimately a good one - to clean and clear the karma of the density of this level of existence in the best way possible.

3) Recognize when something is yours and when it is not. There are so many horrific things happening in your world all the time. And that certainly is not going to stop any time soon if ever.

Therefore, it is extremely easy to get "rolled over" or hit in the face over and over and over again by the tragic and truly horrific things that are happening and have happened on your planet throughout the life of humans on the planet. This is not going to go away. However, what we would like to invite you to do is to - again - take a LOT of deep breaths. Give yourself space to not be stuck in the muck and the mire of every single tragic thing that is happening on the planet at all times. This is not helpful to you or to anyone or anything you care about, including the people, places, things, and entities directly affected by the traumas and atrocities that you are upset about. In fact, you certainly came to the planet to help and to be of service in this great time of shifting and great time of need. However, you came to help in a particular way. You did not come to change or help every single orphan or clean every single stream or heal every single broken heart. You came to help in the way you came to help. Some is yours to do and most is NOT. So please remember this. We invite you to get very still and quiet and to find the inner voice in you that knows exactly what you came to do and knows exactly what is "yours to do" and what is not. The wisdom is all in you. If you need or want assistance with this, please find more help in our Sacred Soul Remembrance online experience at the Living the One Light website.

4) Create space. Create sacred spaces. Create space in yourself. Create space in your life. Create time and be out in real nature. Remember the natural world, for real. This is real life. The tragedies on Earth are real. They are very important. And at the same time, in the reality of the stars and of the planets and of the comets, there is no such thing as anything being less than perfect and whole and in a complete healing state. Therefore, one of the most crucial and healing things you can do is to simply be in nature and to go into and remember your cosmic realities and

your oneness with the all that is. Remember the perfect, whole, healing and healed state that IS you, that IS the cosmos, that IS the stars and the dance between the sun and the Earth and the moon. We have created many free resources for remembering these realities in the channeled videos at the Living the One Light Youtube channel. We invite you to return to these again and again. In particular, we invite you to use the videos regarding "A World with No Fear" and "You Are Whole" as visceral reminders of these states of being. You ARE whole, you ARE perfect. You ARE safe in the ultimate sense. And remembering this all is crucial in navigating even what might be very difficult or challenging times.

5) Practice balance, express all of who you are, and HAVE FUN!!! So as we said above, part of what we do love about your concepts of astrology and of the zodiac is that while it is a funny construct to us in a way, it has allowed you all to flesh out various parts of yourselves. Part of what has happened in your time of density is that most of you have forgotten most of yourselves! For example, most of you have lived into one or two or three aspects of yourselves and have forgotten that you are not only, let's say a sweet, nurturing, grounded, hard working being, but that you ALSO, AT THE SAME TIME are a goddess warrior who is deeply sexual, passionate, angry, fiery, sometimes flighty, sometimes playful and funny, sometimes lost in the stars, sometimes creative and juicy, sometimes profane, sometimes sacred. You are EVERYTHING!!! LITERALLY!!! And we invite you to have SO MUCH FUN with the ALL THAT YOU ARE and the ALL THAT IS!!! In this time of the shifting of this seesaw, the shifting and dredging out of this karmic density and guck, one of the most healing and best ways to lighten things up is literally to lighten up! Have fun! Laugh! Be the warrior. Be the bull. Be the flighty, geeky nerd. Be the inner, vulnerable

child who needs to held and to cry. Be the Leo lion queen or king on the stage. Be the hard working, meticulous, beautiful Virgo. Be the balancer, the reciprocal Libra. Be ALL the ways of being and truly just soak it all in and ENJOY!!!!

6) Sing... open song in your body. Open all forms of resonance and vibration to move through you. Singing and all forms of music are vibration. For that matter, laughing, poetry, any voice that comes through from your deepest, most true place is a way of connecting with your truest self, your purest values. Let the sounds flow... and also DANCE. Just sing and dance and flow...

7) Connect to the All that Is. Similar to #5 above, simply take time to connect to your highest self every day - sometimes multiple times per day. The most helpful thing you can do to navigate any situations that may feel difficult or overwhelming is to connect to a higher version of yourself. In times of true crisis, this may be the best solution or you may need to connect to a higher reality of love with another. You may need a hug or a reminder that you are held and loved and cared about on a human level. But short of an immediate, true crisis (and sometimes even in the midst of one), coming back to the reality of the All That Is, the reality that you are a being in the midst of literally the vast expanse of infinity, can often help to ground you in a much higher perspective and help you to come back to who you truly are and why you came to this planet in the first place. We offer many free healing and healed state that IS you, that IS the cosmos, that IS the stars and the dance between the sun and the Earth and the moon. We have created many free resources for remembering these realities in the channeled videos at the Living the One Light Youtube channel. We invite you to return to these again and again. In particular, we invite you to use the videos regarding "A

World with No Fear" and "You Are Whole" as visceral reminders of these states of being. You ARE whole, you ARE perfect. You ARE safe in the ultimate sense. And remembering this all is crucial in navigating even what might be very difficult or challenging times.

5) Practice balance, express all of who you are, and HAVE FUN!!! So as we said above, part of what we do love about your concepts of astrology and of the zodiac is that while it is a funny construct to us in a way, it has allowed you all to flesh out various parts of yourselves. Part of what has happened in your time of density is that most of you have forgotten most of yourselves! For example, most of you have lived into one or two or three aspects of yourselves and have forgotten that you are not only, let's say a sweet, nurturing, grounded, hard working being, but that you ALSO, AT THE SAME TIME are a goddess warrior who is deeply sexual, passionate, angry, fiery, sometimes flighty, sometimes playful and funny, sometimes lost in the stars, sometimes creative and juicy, sometimes profane, sometimes sacred. You are EVERYTHING!!! LITERALLY!!! And we invite you to have SO MUCH FUN with the ALL THAT YOU ARE and the ALL THAT IS!!! In this time of the shifting of this seesaw, the shifting and dredging out of this karmic density and guck, one of the most healing and best ways to lighten things up is literally to lighten up! Have fun! Laugh! Be the warrior. Be the bull. Be the flighty, geeky nerd. Be the inner, vulnerable child who needs to held and to cry. Be the Leo lion queen or king on the stage. Be the hard working, meticulous, beautiful Virgo. Be the balancer, the reciprocal Libra. Be ALL the ways of being and truly just soak it all in and ENJOY!!!!

6) Sing... open song in your body. Open all forms of

resonance and vibration to move through you. Singing and all forms of music are vibration. For that matter, laughing, poetry, any voice that comes through from your deepest, most true place is a way of connecting with your truest self, your purest values. Let the sounds flow... and also DANCE. Just sing and dance and flow...

7) Connect to the All that Is. Similar to #5 above, simply take time to connect to your highest self every day - sometimes multiple times per day. The most helpful thing you can do to navigate any situations that may feel difficult or overwhelming is to connect to a higher version of yourself. In times of true crisis, this may be the best solution or you may need to connect to a higher reality of love with another. You may need a hug or a reminder that you are held and loved and cared about on a human level. But short of an immediate, true crisis (and sometimes even in the midst of one), coming back to the reality of the All That Is, the reality that you are a being in the midst of literally the vast expanse of infinity, can often help to ground you in a much higher perspective and help you to come back to who you truly are and why you came to this planet in the first place. We offer many free meditations that take you to this place at www.livingtheonelight.com and our Youtube channel. Please connect with those meditations any time you like.

8) As you connect to your highest truth, Envision and Create the World You See in your highest self. The reality of this "new way" that your human world is moving into and moving toward is not set in stone. There are energies that are moving and that give the "new way" potentialities and possibilities and opportunities to be certain ways, but the reality of how it moves and manifests will come through you. You are on the planet to allow these manifesting energies to move through you, ideally through the

love and light and beauty that you came to shine and create with in this lifetime. So we can not lay out "how the world will be" because that is really a matter of choice by all of you. However, we would like to share some ideas of how the energies could manifest should you choose.

POSSIBLE COMPONENTS OF A NEW WAY AND A NEW ORDER

So here are the some ways in which we see that you all could choose to move into a new way of being, especially given the shift in energies that is moving through all of existence and affecting your end of things. These are just a beginning of the possibilities. As we say below, the possibilities are truly endless and only you will know how they could all manifest. Here are some thoughts to get you started in visioning and constructing what you came here to make happen.

All Possibilities Open Up: As the energies of existence start to tilt and move and lighten up the density in your world, all kinds of possibilities open up and lighten up. As you allow your beings to open up with the energies, you will be filled with ideas and new ways of being and doing that you could never have imagined. Just go with this.

Power Structures Even Out: Again, as the energies of things open up and even out, all power structures will also open up and even out and become much more equal and fair. When there is a sense of freedom and openness and lightness, the equality and value of all beings, all creatures, all people will become much more apparent, and egalitarian ways of operating will seem much more natural and comfortable and obvious.

Wisdom Comes Through Everything and Everyone:
Similar to the second point above, as the value of each being
becomes more apparent and obvious and cherished, the truth and
reality that the wisdom of the All that Is comes through every
creature and every person will also become incredibly obvious and
apparent.

Wisdom Comes From Within: As each person and being
and creature is truly valued and held in reverence and respect, each
being and person will suddenly discover the truth that their hearts
and their souls and their bodies and their minds are instruments
of the highest wisdom of existence. The voice of the divine will
suddenly start to speak through each person and each being and
all of the puzzle pieces of what is needed next or what is needed
to be known will suddenly become much more clear as more and
more of the puzzle pieces are shared through every creature they
are meant to be shared through.

We Are Balances of Each Other: Another truth that
will become much more obvious the more and more that these
energies shift and as each person and creature is truly loved and
appreciated is that we are each balances of each other. We are
each mirrors and in right order with each other. The perception
that we are dualistic or dichotomized or "him" or "her" or that we
are one side of a pole versus another one will start to no longer
make sense. Along these lines, the schism and hurts and pains of
the "masculine" versus the "feminine" will begin to even out. The
masculine energies will start to embrace the feminine energies.
The feminine energies will embrace the masculine energies. We
will be an interwoven yin and yang, beautiful spiral and dance in
love with each other and within ourselves. The masculine will love
and cherish and feel the pain of the feminine. The feminine will
love and cherish and feel the pain of the masculine. The two will

remember the dance of all things that says that they are actually one and the same and that they only separated to do a dance with each other, but that that dance has gone awry and now it is time to remember each other fully and completely and to forgive and forgive and forgive and to love and love and love.

We Are ALL Energies of the All that Is: Similar to this last point above, we will remember that we are all energies of all that is. We are not one end of a spectrum of something or one polarity of another thing. We are EVERYTHING. Literally. As these energies open up and we open up, we will begin to realize that we really are all of everything and we will begin to remember the freedom and juiciness and importance of allowing all aspects of life to express through ourselves. We will remember what it is to stretch and grow and be free in all of who we are, even beyond who we thought we could be or would ever be. This is part of us allowing through the wisdom and the puzzle pieces that are needed by the collective to come through us.

It is fun and important to remember the energies in each of us that are serious, studious, responsible, fun loving, sexual, sensual, angry, beautiful, deeply painful, vulnerable, open, closed, hard, soft, receptive, penetrating, adorable, adoring, sharing, boundaried, quiet, loud, heard, deeply hearing, protective, protected, nurturing, held, grounded, stable, flighty, changing, teaching, learning, theatrical, seen, clean, messy, discerning, balanced, harmonious, needy, merged, separate, exploring, cocooning, structured, organized, productive, innovative, gregarious, ahead of the times, traditional, ethereal, divine, earthly. One aspect of the expression of energies in your astrological constructs is that it allows you to explore all aspects of various archetypes. And the key thing about these archetypes is that they are ALL you. We would like to elaborate a bit on this here:

A NOTE ABOUT ARCHETYPES

Archetypes are ways in which humans have attempted to categorize, to flesh out, to embody, and to make sense of all of the various ways of being on this planet. Archetypes can be extremely helpful if approached in a particular way. They are expressions of ALL of you. As we noted above, you are not simply "an Aries" warrior or "a Virgo" hardworking goddess. Your true nature is ALL of existence, so a very positive use of archetypes is to remember that they ALL exist in you. The ultimate purpose of coming to this planet is certainly to help, but also to stretch into and remember all parts of existence and all parts of YOU and then to come back into balance of all of these energies.

So, for example, in your astrological terminologies, you might talk about a warrior energy being related to the constellation and energies of Aries. You might talk about the energy of groundedness and stability being associated with Taurus. And this is wonderful in that it allows you to externalize and therefore remember and exercise those various aspects of yourselves. What we want to caution against, however, is any sense or notion that you are anything other than ALL of these archetypes all at the same time. There is no such thing as a person who "is a Taurus" or who "is an Aries." All of existence is all of EVERYTHING, yes? And you are literally made up of the substance of all of existence, so therefore, you are everything! And we would like to encourage you to try on, remember, stretch into, and grow through ALL of these archetypes, ALL of these energies, ALL of these ways of being. And this is part of the beauty of the cycles of life on your planet, in your universe, in your galaxy, in your solar system, in your cells, in yourself! You are constantly moving through time, constantly moving through space, constantly rotating and moving and changing and growing and adapting as everything moves and grows and changes throughout life itself.

And ultimately, we would love for you to remember that in your moving through all of these archetypes, the ultimate goal is to try them all out, feel them all out, re-become each of them, and ultimately to come to a balance of all of them in yourself, in our world, in our being-ness throughout existence, and ultimately to dissolve back into the perfectly balanced world of the all that is.

So... in this journal, laugh, love, explore, HAVE FUN, try on parts of yourselves that maybe you have forgotten or that maybe you have been ashamed or scared of or that maybe you were told not to be. Remember your warrior self, remember your grounded, sensual self, remember your bouncy, gregarious self, remember your deep, soulful, painful side, remember your expansive, all knowing, cosmic intuition, remember your quick, funny wit, remember your cuddly, nurturing side. Remember and relax into ALL of who you are and ENJOY....

And on that note, next we will now explain the gist of the archetypes of the zodiac... the various aspects of ALL of who you are!!!

Thank you for listening, thank you for being here, and so much love...

THE ARCHETYPES OF THE ZODIAC

Like we have said above, the reality of existence is so far beyond anything that can be captured in any human words or concepts. So the same applies to the concepts of astrology and the archetypes of the zodiac. And even within the constructs of the zodiac, there is a huge range and variety and complexity and richness in each of these archetypes. So what we are giving you here is simply a nugget, a starting place for you to feel into each of these energies over time and for you to start to explore and get to know this part of life and these parts of yourself.

In western astrology, there are twelve "signs" or twelve archetypes of the zodiac. They are as follows:

Aries: Aries is ruled by the planet Mars. Aries is the warrior, the god of war. Aries is fire and "go get 'em" nature. Aries is drive and instinct. Aries charges ahead and penetrates. Aries is a spark that kicks you out of bed and says, "On with it!" Aries gets things started and can catalyze change.

Taurus: Taurus is ruled by the planet Venus. Taurus is "the bull." Taurus is the grounded, sensual nature of home and clothing and textures. Taurus likes being fixed and earthy. Taurus loves to curl up with a book and stay cozy in a warm bed. Taurus is sensual and sexual in the physical world. Taurus loves beautiful things and loves to be held and touched. Taurus loves a good massage and the smell of gorgeous flowers and the sun on the skin. Taurus is steady and true.

Gemini: Gemini is ruled by the planet Mercury. Gemini is a communicator. Gemini loves to talk and think and speak and write and say whatever is on its mind. Gemini loves to learn and has to do with childhood, siblings, and primary school. Gemini can think fast, is an air sign, and can be flighty, moving from thing to thing to thing to thing. Gemini is often curious and inquisitive. Gemini can be dualistic and secretive. Gemini can also be a great explainer of details and important information. Gemini is a great energy for helping the world to understand many things better.

Cancer: Cancer is ruled by the Moon. Similar to the moon, cancer is often sweet and sensitive. Cancer is the sign of the mother and childhood. Cancer is the most vulnerable and inner part of oneself. Cancer is the most raw, truth of who we are deep down, the part of us that needs to be treated tenderly and with honor and great care. Cancer can be watery and emotional, with ups and downs changing in rapid pace. Cancer has great wisdom in what we truly need and can speak purely if we listen with great quiet.

Leo: Leo is ruled by the Sun. Leo is the king, the queen, the lion, the lioness. Leo is on the stage and loves to be the center of attention. Leo needs to be witnessed and praised. Leo has a big heart and loves to shine and to be seen in that shining way. Leo is creative and relates to all that we create, including our children. Leo can be very loving and also somewhat self centered at times. Leo is expression of all kinds in warm and wonderful ways that need to be seen and need to be shared in our world.

Virgo: Virgo is ruled by Mercury, just like Gemini. Virgo is beautiful. Virgo is discriminating. Virgo can be a true healer. Virgo is down to earth and practical. Virgo is diligent and works hard. Virgo is persistent and methodical. Virgo is self contained and perceptive. Virgo is clean and clears out what is no longer needed. Virgo is reliable and true.

Libra: Libra is ruled by Venus, just as Taurus is. Libra is a kind of beauty, slightly different in quality from earthy, beautiful Virgo. Libra is balanced and in tune with the other. Libra is the sign related to partnerships of all kinds, of working and balancing with the others, including in marriage partnerships. Libra likes harmony and can be co-dependent. Libra often needs to balance with its polarity of Aries to learn to be independent while also interdependent. Libra is a wonderful listener and can truly understand all sides of a situation. Libra is a great mediator and friend.

Scorpio: Scorpio is ruled by the planet Pluto and historically ruled by Mars. Scorpio is deep and dark. Scorpio is related to the underworld, the areas of depth and death that people often are afraid of. Scorpio is incredibly perceptive and likes to bring up and talk about things that often get left unsaid or unnamed. Scorpio is the taboo. Scorpio is death. Scorpio is the deep healer, the medicine man and medicine woman, the sage, the elder of the deep, the shaman. Scorpio has a deep magic and incredible power. Scorpio helps things to die over and over and over again and is crucial in assisting us to let go of anything that is no longer serving the deepest, most true evolution of our soul.

Sagittarius: Sagittarius is ruled by Jupiter. Sagittarius is big and boisterous and expansive. Sagittarius is the leader, teacher, guru. Sagittarius is the big, wide world, the explorer energy, the part of us that wants to go and try out new foods, new ways, immerse in new languages and places and perhaps become something that we never thought we could be before. Sagittarius is the "foreign." Sagittarius is luck and exaggeration at the same time. Sagittarius has to do with beliefs and religion and sometimes dogma. Sagittarius has to do with truth and can sometimes stretch the truth. Sagittarius can help us to discern our own truth and to speak it to the world.

Capricorn: Capricorn is ruled by Saturn. Capricorn is the elder leader CEO. Capricorn is the energy that tells us "how things should be." Capricorn is the structures of society that we feel are set in stone. Capricorn rules the bones and is dense and sometimes hard. Capricorn can be a great or harsh task master. Capricorn is excellent at knowing and setting and reminding us of boundaries and time and space. Capricorn gets things done, similar to Virgo, but in a more top down way, as opposed to the methodical, internally driven nature of Virgo. Capricorn can represent the patriarchy, the ways things "have been done" and can be dominating or domineering. At the same time, Capricorn can give a structure to our ideas and passions and can help us to manifest in concrete ways. Capricorn can give us great strength in remembering our own internal leader and boss and our own ability to move ahead and do what we came to do.

Aquarius: Aquarius is ruled by the planet Uranus. Aquarius is innovation. Aquarius is the future. Aquarius moves quickly and is fast and in the realm of the genius and the cosmic. Aquarius comes up with brilliant new ideas and cares a great deal about the collective good. Aquarius is groups and friendships. Aquarius is beautiful and airy and analytical. Aquarius is visionary and can show us things literally of the stars.

Pisces: Pisces is ruled by the planet Neptune and historically by Jupiter. Pisces is the sign of the All that Is. Pisces is ether and the chaos and all knowingness of everything. Pisces is all of existence. Pisces is our intuition, our knowing and divinity and purest love through our hearts. Pisces is the ethereal. Pisces can be related to addiction and depression and despondency. Pisces can help us to channel what needs to come through from all of existence, the spirit world, and the energies of all things. Pisces is beautiful in its own divine way and reminds us that we are all truly one.

COSMIC CYCLES

One fun way to explore the energies of existence as expressed in these archetypes is by following the cycles of the cosmos and the astrological phenomena of the year.

As is likely obvious, in reality, there are an infinite number of cycles in the cosmos. There are far more than anyone can imagine and they keep changing and growing and becoming new over and over and over again.

So for the purposes of this journal, we will simply highlight a few that might be a helpful place for you to start to tap into and notice the rhythms in your sky and in your self. Those include the cycles of the moon (the new moon and full moon), the lunar and solar eclipses, and some general notes about the astrological configurations of the year of 2020.

MOON CYCLES

Do you know your moon? Do you watch your moon? Do you know and remember the beautiful balance and friendship that your moon has between your planet Earth and your sun and you, for that matter? Your moon is in a constant dance and balance of rhythms and movement and cycles constantly with you, with your body, with the earth, with her oceans, with her plants, with all beings in, on, and around her body. The moon is a beautiful being, in and of herself. And what an opportunity you have in your time on Earth to fully remember and embrace your relationship to your moon. She is your friend. Look up and smile and feel her embrace...

The moon can represent so many energies, so we will highlight a few to get your own internal knowing and your own truths ignited. Feel into the energy of the moon and your own relationship with her and she will speak to and through you and you will know what truths are in sync with your own reality of who she is and who you are and what she is here to guide you in.

In general, however, the moon is often thought of as a mirror of our internal world, our inner most beautiful and vulnerable selves, our inner child, and also our inner mother. It represents our need to be held and nurtured and our ability and desire to hold and nurture ourselves and others as well. The moon can be a reflection of our literal home, our figurative homes, our home inside ourselves, our home in wherever we are. The moon can represent our actual mother. The moon can represent anyone or anything that gave or gives us unconditional love, including ourselves. The moon can be a reflection of our inner world, unfiltered, and so much more. Let the moon talk with you, let her reflect for you. Open up and remember who the moon is for you, right here, right now, and in each moment. She has watched you and been present for you in every moment of existence of this planet. Literally. Just sink in and let her flow....

NEW MOONS

New moons are a time when the sun and the moon are conjunct in the sky - they come together in their dance around and with your earth. The new moon is a time when there is energy for starting new, for starting fresh, for going deep inside yourself and for clicking in with what is truly right and good and best for the real you, the inner most you, the most vulnerable and raw and honest you. Typically, this is a wonderful time for "setting intentions" and for getting clear on your most real, inner truth, and what it is that is right and best for the real you.

FULL MOONS

Full moons are when there is an energy of fullness, of ripeness, when our inner light can shine and be reflected in its full glory and beauty and when our intentions of the new moons can come to fruition. This can happen in many ways. As we said above, there are many rhythms in life and in the cosmos. When you set an intention on a new moon, the intentions flow out into the world and will ripple and come back around in waves that you can not know and can not predict. However, we invite you to notice and observe the effects of those intentions in two main ways:

The Four Week New Moon to New Moon Cycle

First, notice the energy of that intention as it builds over the following two weeks to the next full moon. For example, if you set an intention on the new moon in Aquarius on January 24, 2020, notice how the energies of that intention may build and/or come to fruition in some way at the full moon two weeks later in Leo on February 8, 2020, and then how that energy might close at the next new moon which happens in Pisces on February 23, 2020. We focus on this cycle in this journal as a place to start noticing cycles and movements of energy in your life.

The Full Year New Moon to New Moon Cycle

Second, notice the energy that you might observe of a particular intention throughout a yearly cycle of a new moon in a particular sign to a new moon approximately a year later in that same sign. So, for example, start to observe what might occur regarding an intention you set on the new moon in Aquarius on January 24, 2020, how that might culminate at the next FULL moon in Aquarius on August 3, 2020, and then come to completion at the next NEW moon in Aquarius on February 11,

2021. We do not focus on that cycle in this journal this year, but we want to make note of it so that you can notice this cycle as well if that feels right for you.

ECLIPSES

Eclipses are portals. Eclipses are a time of beautiful, incredible opportunity for certain energies to flow through to the collective unconscious. They are also an opportunity for you to ride into the wave of those energies consciously and for you to allow your life to be transformed in powerful ways that are supported through the energies of the eclipse. Like any other energies, eclipses often bring change that will happen one way or another, regardless of whether a person is conscious of what is happening. However, if you are able to be aware and strategically get behind the wave, you can follow the energies into your life with grace and ease and power like never before when you were not conscious of them.

OTHER MAJOR ASPECTS OF 2020

As we mentioned above, there are some major aspects of 2020 that involve Pluto, Saturn, Jupiter, and the south node of the moon conjunct in the sign of Capricorn. These aspects are very significant energetically as we described above.

In addition, the nodes of the moon will move from Capricorn and Cancer into Sagittarius and Gemini on May 5, 2020. This is also a significant shift of a collective focus moving from the inner world of Cancer to the curious, communicative sign of Gemini.

We want to highlight what we mention above that Saturn and Jupiter will conjunct each other at 0 degrees of Aquarius on the winter solstice, December 21, 2020. Many astrologers are calling this conjunction "the beginning of the Age of Aquarius." We simply would like to note that it is a significant moment of energies coming together who could be able to kick off a confluence of events and energies that could help you to propel your world into the light and airy and innovative and egalitarian world that you might be choosing to envision and to begin to structure of the course of 2020. We hope and invite you to use these energies to the best of your abilities, to ride these waves into yourselves and to ride the waves as a collective in a way that is the most aligned and in highest truth of your souls and your selves.

In addition, Venus and Mars will both go retrograde during this year, as will Mercury and other planets as well. We note throughout the year how the energies of each transit, including these retrogrades, have the potential to be perfect supports and energetic assistants to the overall goal of transformation and healing on the planet. It is actually quite amazing and beautiful how the intricate, complex, and multi-faceted moving pieces of your solar system truly do play into a perfectly choreographed dance and song that can only truly be conceived by the divine.

With that, we bless you, we bless your year, we bless your time as you move forward and as you navigate these changing tides. We love you and we thank you for being on this planet right here and right now.

We are always here to support you, to guide you, to remind you of the All That Is and the All that is YOU.

So much love...

Basic COSMIC RHYTHMS of 2019

January 5, 2019, 5:28pm, PST - New Moon in Capricorn, 15 degrees, 24'

    - Partial Solar Eclipse, 5:42pm, PST, 15 degrees, 31'

January 20, 2019, 9:15pm, PST - Full Moon in Leo, 0 degrees, 50'
    - Total Lunar Eclipse, 9:13pm, PST, 0 degrees, 49'

February 4, 2019, 1:03pm, PST - New Moon in Aquarius, 15 degrees, 44'

February 19, 2019, 7:53am, PST - Full Moon in Virgo, 0 degrees, 42'

March 6, 2019, 8:03am, PST - New Moon in Pisces, 15 degrees, 46'

March 20, 2019, 8:03am, PST - Full Moon in Libra, 0 degrees, 08'

April 5, 2019, 1:50am, PST - New Moon in Aries, 15 degrees, 16'

April 19, 2019, 4:12am, PST - Full Moon in Libra, 29 degrees, 06'

May 4, 2019, 3:45pm, PST - New Moon in Taurus, 14 degrees, 10'

May 18, 2019, 2:11pm, PST - Full Moon in Scorpio, 27 degrees, 38'

June 3, 2019, 3:01am, PST - New Moon in Gemini, 12 degrees, 33'

June 17, 2019, 1:30am, PST - Full Moon in Sagittarius, 25 degrees, 52'

July 2, 2019, 12:16pm, PST - New Moon in Cancer, 10 degrees, 37'

       - Total Solar Eclipse, 10 degrees, 42'

July 16, 2019, 2:38pm, PST - Full Moon in Capricorn, 24 degrees, 04'

       - Partial Lunar Eclipse, 24 degrees, 00'

July 31, 2019, 8:11pm, PST - New Moon in Leo, 8 degrees, 36'

August 15, 2019, 5:29am, PST - Full Moon in Aquarius, 22 degrees, 24'

August 30, 2019, 3:37am, PST - New Moon in Virgo, 6 degrees, 46'

September 13, 2019, 9:32pm, PST - Full Moon in Pisces, 21 degrees, 04'

September 28, 2019, 11:26am, PST - New Moon in Libra, 5 degrees, 19'

October 13, 2019, 2:07pm, PST - Full Moon in Aries, 20 degrees, 13'

October 27, 2019, 8:38pm, PST - New Moon in Scorpio, 4 degrees, 24'

November 12, 2019, 5:34am, PST - Full Moon in Taurus, 19 degrees, 51'

November 26, 2019, 7:05am, PST - New Moon in Sagittarius, 4 degrees, 02'

December 11, 2019, 9:12pm, PST - Full Moon in Gemini, 19 degrees, 51'

December 25, 2019, 9:12pm, PST - New Moon in Capricorn, 4 degrees, 06'
- Solar Eclipse, 4 degrees, 09'

COSMIC RHYTHMS of 2020

Friday, January 10, 2020, 11:21am, PST - Full Moon in Cancer, 20 degrees 00'

- Lunar Eclipse, 11:11am, PST, 19 degrees, 54' with Jupiter on the South Node in Capricorn

- Uranus stations direct at 2 degrees Taurus

Sunday, January 12, 2020 - SATURN AND PLUTO CONJUNCTION in Capricorn, along with Ceres, Sun, and Mercury

Friday, January 24, 2020, 1:41pm, PST - New Moon in Aquarius, 4 degrees 21'

Saturday, February 8, 2020, 11:33pm, PST - Full Moon in Leo, 20 degrees, 00'

Sunday, February 16, 2020 - Mercury Goes Retrograde at 12 degrees Pisces

Sunday, February 23, 2020, 7:31am, PST - New Moon in Pisces, 4 degrees, 28'

Monday, March 9, 2020, 10:47am, PST - Full Moon in Virgo, 19 degrees, 36'

- Mercury Goes Direct at 28 Degrees Aquarius

Saturday, March 21, 2020 - Saturn Enters Aquarius

Tuesday, March 24, 2020, 2:28am, PST - New Moon in Aries, 4 degrees, 12'

Saturday, April 4, 2020 - JUPITER AND PLUTO CONJUNCTION at 24 degrees Capricorn

Tuesday, April 7, 2020, 7:34pm, PST - Full Moon in Libra, 18 degrees, 42'

Wednesday, April 22, 2020, 7:25pm, PST - New Moon in Taurus, 3 degrees, 23'

Wednesday, May 6, 2020 - NORTH NODE OF THE MOON ENTERS GEMINI; SOUTH NODE ENTERS SAGITTARIUS (and stay until January 18, 2022)

Thursday, May 7, 2020, 3:45am, PST - Full Moon in Scorpio, 17 degrees, 19'

Sunday, May 10, 2020 - Saturn goes Retrograde at 1 degree Aquarius

Wednesday, May 13, 2020 - Venus Goes Retrograde at 22 degrees Gemini

Thursday, May 14, 2020 - JUPITER GOES RETROGRADE at 27 degrees Capricorn

Friday, May 22, 2020, 10:38am, PST - New Moon in Gemini, 2 degrees, 04'

Friday, June 5, 2020, 12:12pm, PST - Full Moon in Sagittarius, 15 degrees, 33'
- Lunar Eclipse, 12:26pm, PST, 15 degrees, 42', Sun and Venus nearly conjunct in Gemini

Thursday, June 18, 2020 - Mercury Goes Retrograde at 14 degrees Cancer

Saturday, June 20, 2020, 11:41pm, PST - New Moon in Cancer, 0 degrees, 21'
- Annular Solar Eclipse, 11:41pm, PST, 0 degrees

Friday, June 26, 2020 - Venus Stations Direct at 6 degrees Gemini

Tuesday, June 30, 2020 - JUPITER AND PLUTO CONJUNCTION (Second time) at 24 degrees Capricorn

Wednesday, July 1, 2020 - Saturn re-enters Capricorn going retrograde

Saturday, July 4, 2020, 9:44pm, PST - Full Moon in Capricorn, 13 degrees, 37'

- Lunar Eclipse, 9:31pm, PST, 13 degrees, 30'

Sunday, July 12, 2020 - Mercury Goes Direct at 5 degrees Cancer

Monday, July 20, 2020, 10:32am, PST - New Moon in Cancer, 28 degrees, 26'

Monday, August 3, 2020, 8:58am, PST - Full Moon in Aquarius, 11 degrees, 45'

Tuesday, August 18, 2020, 7:41pm, PST - New Moon in Leo, 26 degrees, 34'

Tuesday, September 1, 2020, 10:21pm, PST - Full Moon in Pisces, 10 degrees, 11'

Wednesday, September 9, 2020 - Mars Goes Retrograde at 28 degrees Aries

Saturday, September 12, 2020 - Jupiter Stations Direct at 25 degrees Capricorn

Thursday, September 17, 2020, 4:00am, PST - New Moon in Virgo, 25 degrees, 00'

Monday, September 28, 2020 - Saturn Stations Direct at 25 degrees Capricorn

Thursday, October 1, 2020, 2:05pm, PST - Full Moon in Aries, 9 degrees, 08'

Sunday, October 4, 2020 - Pluto Stations Direct at 22 degrees Capricorn

Tuesday, October 13, 2020 - Mercury Goes Retrograde at 11 degrees Scorpio

Friday, October 16, 2020, 12:30pm, PST - New Moon in Libra, 23 degrees, 52'

Saturday, October 31, 2020, 7:49am, PST - Full Moon in Taurus, 8 degrees, 38'

Tuesday, November 3, 2020 - Mercury Goes Direct at 25 degrees Libra

Thursday, November 12, 2020 - JUPITER AND PLUTO CONJUNCTION (for the THIRD time) at 22 degrees Capricorn

Friday, November 13, 2020 - Mars stations direct at 15 degrees Aries

Saturday, November 14, 2020, 9:07pm, PST - New Moon in Scorpio, 23 degrees, 17'

Monday, November 30, 2020, 1:29am, PST - Full Moon in Gemini, 8 degrees, 37'

- Lunar Eclipse, 1:44pm, PST, 8 degrees, 45'

Monday, December 14, 2020, 8:16am, PST - New Moon in Sagittarius, 23 degrees, 07'

- Total Solar Eclipse, 8:14am, PST, 23 degrees, 06' (Sun, Moon, and Mercury conjunct the South Node in Sagittarius)

Thursday, December 17, 2020 - Saturn Re-enters Aquarius (for the second time in 2020)

Saturday, December 19, 2020 - Jupiter Enters Aquarius

Monday, December 21, 2020 - JUPITER AND SATURN CONJUNCTION, 0 degrees, 29 minutes Aquarius

Tuesday, December 29, 2020, 7:28pm, PST - Full Moon in Cancer, 8 degrees, 53'

Basic COSMIC RHYTHMS of 2021

January 12, 2021, 9:00pm, PST - New Moon in Capricorn, 23 degrees, 13'

January 28, 2021, 11:16am, PST - Full Moon in Leo, 20 degrees, 00'

February 11, 2021, 11:05am, PST - New Moon in Aquarius, 23 degrees, 16'

February 27, 2021, 12:17am, PST - Full Moon in Virgo, 8 degrees, 57'

March 13, 2021, 2:21am, PST - New Moon in Pisces, 23 degrees, 03'

March 28, 2021, 11:48am, PST - Full Moon in Libra, 8 degrees, 18'

April 11, 2021, 7:30pm, PST - New Moon in Aries, 22 degrees, 24'

April 26, 2021, 8:31pm, PST - Full Moon in Scorpio, 7 degrees, 05'

May 11, 2021, 11:59am, PST - New Moon in Taurus, 21 degrees, 17'

May 26, 2021, 4:13am, PST - Full Moon in Sagittarius, 5 degrees, 25'
  - Total Lunar Eclipse, 4:19pm, PST, 5 degrees, 29'

June 10, 2021, 3:52am, PST - New Moon in Gemini, 19 degrees, 46'
  - Annular Solar Eclipse, 3:43am, 19 degrees, 42'

June 24, 2021, 11:39am, PST - Full Moon in Capricorn, 3 degrees, 27'

July 9, 2021, 6:16pm, PST - New Moon in Cancer, 18 degrees, 01'

July 23, 2021, 7:36pm, PST - Full Moon in Aquarius, 1 degrees, 25'

August 8, 2021, 6:49am, PST - New Moon in Leo, 16 degrees, 13'

August 22, 2021, 5:01am, PST - Full Moon in Aquarius, 29 degrees, 36'

September 6, 2021, 5:51pm, PST - New Moon in Virgo, 14 degrees, 37'

September 20, 2021, 4:54pm, PST - Full Moon in Pisces, 28 degrees, 13'

October 6, 2021, 4:05am, PST - New Moon in Libra, 13 degrees, 24'

October 20, 2021, 7:56am, PST - Full Moon in Aries, 27 degrees, 25'

November 4, 2021, 2:14pm, PST - New Moon in Scorpio, 12 degrees, 39'

November 19, 2021, 12:57am, PST - Full Moon in Taurus, 27 degrees, 14'

December 3, 2021, 11:42pm, PST - New Moon in Sagittarius, 12 degrees, 21'
    - Total Solar Eclipse, 11:34pm, PST, 12 degrees, 16'

December 18, 2021, 8:35pm, PST - Full Moon in Gemini, 27 degrees, 28'

JOURNAL

PAGES

A BLESSING AND REMINDER

As you begin journaling, we would like to take a minute again to bless your process and to give you a couple of reminders.

1) This is YOUR journal. This is YOUR life. Your life is yours. Your reality is yours. Your soul is your own. What is meant to come through you is meant to come through YOU. So we have provided some information and context for each of the dates we describe over the course of the year. However, on each of those dates, some or none or all might feel relevant or be helpful or apply to YOUR day, your life, and what is manifesting and needing to move through you in that moment. Please ignore, change, augment, and/or flow with what is written here exactly as feels right for you in a given moment.

2) To that end, we will start each of these dates with space for you to first drop in and get clear for yourself on what is coming up for you, what is present for you, and what energies YOUR soul is feeling and focusing on that day. We invite you to first tune into yourself and then read the message we have written for you if that feels best or, again, simply use this journal in exactly whatever way is best for you.

3) Throughout the journal, we provide prompts. This are simply that - prompts. Once again, use them exactly how feels best for you. Let your soul be your guide. You can follow these prompts one by one, in order, exactly as they are given or not! You can write your responses here, you can get a separate blank journal and write responses there. You can draw or paint in response to the prompts. You can simply read through the prompts and feel or pray or meditate and allow and notice the energies and images that come through for you. You can use the prompts as a way of moving conversations between you and loved ones or groups of people in a sacred space. Or any number of endless possiblities...

We bless you, we love you, and we are so glad you are here. May this journal support your sacred life through 2020 and beyond...

ENTERING 2020

Welcome to the cusp of the year 2020!

We would like to give you an opportunity to reflect on where you are coming from, what you are sitting with, what you are bringing into this new year, what you would like to leave behind, and what your intentions are for yourself and your world while moving into 2020.

So with that, simply close your eyes, take a deep, deep breath, connect up to your highest connection of the all that is, and write, draw, allow to move through you whatever comes through. You are beautiful. We are so glad you are here.

At this moment, as I am entering the world of 2020, I am feeling, thinking, believing, knowing….

Up until this point, my journey has been…

I breathe in and feel all things that I do not need falling away….

As I am entering the year 2020, I am surrounded by the support of……

As I enter 2020, I am deeply grateful for…..

As I enter 2020, I ask to be joined by…..

I am joined, supported, and held by the All That Is and I
envision….

My most sacred intentions moving into this year and the rest of my life are…

While I am journeying in this year, I would like for myself to remember and to be reminded that…

And so it is.

WEDNESDAY, DECEMBER 25, 2019

NEW MOON IN CAPRICORN, 4 degrees, 9:14pm, PST
SOLAR ECLIPSE in Capricorn

Getting Centered in You

We invite you to start by taking a deep breath, dropping into your true center, your beautiful and pure soul. And from this place, name what is true for you...

Today, I am feeling...

In this moment, what is present for me is...

Today, I am needing...

Today, mine to do is...

Our Message for You

And now we invite you to let wash over you as feels right this message about the energies present today...

Today holds the transit that sets the tone for the year of 2020. Today is a new moon solar eclipse at 4 degrees of Capricorn. This is highly appropriate given all of the energies of the year 2019 and going into 2020.

Today, the energies of the solar system as a whole are massive. We will list them because they are so significant, but if they seem confusing, just let these words wash over you and simply feel whatever energies come through for you in them.

The following planets are all grouped together in the sky at the moment: The sun and moon are at 4 degrees Capricorn, next to Jupiter who is at 5 degrees Capricorn. Next is the south node of the moon at 6 degrees Capricorn. After a nine degree break, Ceres is at 15 degrees Capricorn, then Saturn is at 20 degrees Capricorn and Pluto is at 22 degrees Capricorn. In other words, all in Capricorn today are: the moon, the sun, Jupiter, the south node of the moon, Ceres, Saturn, and Pluto. This lends a great deal of power to this solar eclipse in Capricorn as we head into the adventure of 2020.

2020 brings an opportunity to be reviewing, revising, destroying, letting go, and rebuilding many of the energies associated with Capricorn. 2020 also brings an opportunity to harness many of the lessons and gifts and strengths in the energies of Capricorn. So this new moon solar eclipse in Capricorn is a perfect setting for us all to enter the year of 2020 when so much transformation will happen in and with these Capricorn energies.

Today we invite you to simply sit with and feel into the energies of Capricorn - what they mean, what they feel like to you. And we invite you to feel the powerful energies of this eclipse and what changes, what energies it is birthing in you, bringing through for you to go into 2020 as prepared and ready as possible to do a great deal of letting go, transforming re-visioning, and re-creating over the whole year and into the new age moving ahead.

As we mentioned earlier, Capricorn is ruled by Saturn. Capricorn is the elder leader CEO. Capricorn is the energy that tells us "how things should be." Capricorn is the structures of society that we feel are set in stone. Capricorn rules the bones and is dense and sometimes hard. Capricorn can be a great or harsh task master. Capricorn is excellent at knowing and setting and reminding us of boundaries and time and space. Capricorn gets things done, similar to Virgo, but in a more top down way, as opposed to the methodical, internally driven nature of Virgo. Capricorn can represent the patriarchy, the ways things "have been done" and can be dominating or domineering. At the same time, Capricorn can give a structure to our ideas and passions and can help us to manifest in concrete ways. Capricorn can give us great strength in remembering our own internal leader and boss and elder self and our own ability to move ahead and do what we came to do.

The Cosmic Flow Through You

Today, I sit in the new moon in Capricorn which is joined by a powerful set of planets also in the sign of Capricorn. I look forward to the year of 2020 and as I feel these energies of Capricorn, I feel....

Going into 2020, the energies of Capricorn tell me, remind me, want me to take...

I am armed, I am ready, I have all the tools I need as I move forward into this year. I have been prepared, I have done a great deal of work to get to where I am already. I am ready and committed to being present in this year as a midwife, as a visionary, and as a do-er, a creator who is here on this planet right here and right now for exactly this purpose and this time. I feel this and know this and I remember....

Welcome 2020...

FRIDAY, JANUARY 10, 2020

Full Moon in Cancer, 20 degrees 00' - 11:21am, PST

Lunar Eclipse, 11:11am, PST, 19 degrees, 54' with Jupiter on the South Node in Capricorn

Getting Centered in You

We invite you to start by taking a deep breath, dropping into your true center, your beautiful and pure soul. And from this place, name what is true for you...

Today, I am feeling...

In this moment, what is present for me is...

Today, I am needing...

Today, mine to do is...

Our Message for You

Today is the first full moon of the year. The energy of this full moon was initiated on the new moon two weeks ago, on December 25, 2019. Think back to what you were feeling that day or what intentions you may have set either consciously or unconsciously.

This full moon is in Cancer, the sign that is ruled by the moon. A full moon in Cancer can be an opportunity to fully expand and show your inner most vulnerability, to fill up with the acknowledgement that your inner feelings are incredibly valid and important and need to be honored. Cancer can be sensitive, but this sensitivity presents and opportunity to simply sit with, be with, and know what we truly need, feel, and desire in our most true selves. Cancer energy is also associated with our mother, our own mothering, those who have nurtured us, our desire to be nurtured, and our ability to nurture ourselves and others. Cancer can also be associated with our home, our physical house, and a sense of being "cozy" and at home in ourselves.

Also on this day, there is the first lunar eclipse of the year, with the north node of the moon in Cancer and Jupiter conjunct the south node of the moon in Capricorn. This eclipse can bring through many kinds of energies. One is that with Jupiter and the sun in Capricorn conjunct the south node of the moon and the moon opposite in Cancer, this is essentially a kick off of the energies of the year with Jupiter and the sun shining a light on and expanding our ability to unearth the energies of Capricorn in our past - both the positive and challenging aspects of Capricorn.

We then can channel what we want to bring through of the strengths of Capricorn into our ability to hold ourselves in our inner Cancer needs.

The positive aspects of Capricorn can be a great deal of strength, an ability to hold a strong structure and container for things, a strong work ethic and ability to get things done, as well as wisdom and ourselves as the "elder." These are wonderful qualities. The difficult side of Capricorn can be a top down, patriarchal, authoritarian type of energy that is harsh, controlling, and constricting.

So on this day, we invite you to take a deep breath and to feel into these energies, the energies of the moon in your sky, herself. Feel her, see her, hear her move through you whatever energies and wisdom and knowledge she may need you to hear and/or convey. We then invite you to feel specifically into the energies of Cancer and Capricorn and to harness the strengths of both and bring through whatever you may be needing from both and what gifts you are being asked to bring into the world.

Thank you for being the beautiful you…

The Cosmic Flow Through You

I take a deep breath connect to you, beautiful Moon. I feel you and you say…

In this moment of Cancer energies being highlight, I feel….

I bring with me the strength and wisdom of my Capricorn elder self. He or she needs to say….

As I feel the portal and the energy of this eclipse with Jupiter conjunct the south node in Capricorn, I feel the expansion of the energy of Jupiter and I feel myself expanded in my ability to see what needs to stay in the past and what is ready to come through….

The ultimate wisdom of this time and this day is…..

I give gratitude for…..

SATURN AND PLUTO CONJUNCTION

in Capricorn, along with Ceres, Sun, and Mercury

Getting Centered in You

We invite you to start by taking a deep breath, dropping into your true center, your beautiful and pure soul. And from this place, name what is true for you...

Today, I am feeling...

In this moment, what is present for me is...

Today, I am needing...

Today, mine to do is...

Our Message for You

Today is a big day astrologically. This is the first moment of a new cycle between Saturn and Pluto. Saturn is essentially catching up to Pluto and then passing him. It is as though Saturn, the planet regarding our structures, both internally and in society, has completed a long phase and is now hitting Pluto, the planet of deep transformation. This conjunction is happening in Capricorn which is the sign ruled by Saturn. So the overall picture is that this conjunction signifies a moment when we are starting a new phase regarding our inner structures and our structures as a collective. This gives us a chance to start fresh, to release a great deal that no longer serves and to move toward the energy of Aquarius where Saturn is heading next. As we have said before, Aquarius is the sign that brings energies of innovation, thinking "outside of the box," technology, egalitarianism, groups, friendships, and "the good of the collective." So this is a new start, a moment of transformation, a chance to set intentions and to begin to re-envision how we want our selves and our world to approach structure, to approach society, to approach what has been and can be the status quo.

On this day, we invite you to go deep, to feel your deep Pluto soul self, and what needs to transform and shift. We invite you to dive deep into your sense of what structures exist in you, in your relationships, and in your world. Feel into what is working for you and what is needing to transmute, transform. And come to Pluto as a friend of transformation. Look to Saturn as a wisdom keeper, an elder, a wise one who can help you and all of us to identify what structures are working for us all and what is going to be transformed in this cycle coming up over the next many years.

Interestingly, Ceres, the Sun, and Mercury also join this conjunction. So these energies combined are a powerful source of support for us all to not only dive deep, but to also cultivate, shine light, and communicate what we find in the deepest parts of ourselves.

The Cosmic Flow Through You

On this day of this powerful conjunction Pluto, Saturn, Ceres, the Sun, and Mercury in Capricorn, I dive deep into my soul and find the structures that are most significant inside myself and in the world around me. The structures that are being highlighted inside of me today are.......

The aspects of the structures in myself that I feel the need to transform are.....

As I dive deep and come into concert with these beautiful celestial beings, they sing in concert with my soul and the song that comes through says....

FRIDAY, JANUARY 24, 2020

New Moon in Aquarius, 4 degrees 21', 1:41pm, PST

Getting Centered in You

We invite you to start by taking a deep breath, dropping into your true center, your beautiful and pure soul. And from this place, name what is true for you...

Today, I am feeling...

In this moment, what is present for me is...

Today, I am needing...

Today, mine to do is...

Our Message for You

Today is the first new moon in 2020. It is a new moon in Aquarius.

As we stated above, Aquarius is ruled by the planet Uranus. Aquarius is innovation. Aquarius is the future. Aquarius moves quickly and is fast and in the realm of the genius and the cosmic. Aquarius comes up with brilliant new ideas and cares a great deal about the collective good. Aquarius is groups and friendships. Aquarius is beautiful and airy and analytical. Aquarius is visionary and can show us things literally of the stars.

A new moon in Aquarius is a chance to set new intentions, especially regarding the energies associated with these Aquarian qualities. This is highly appropriate given the bigger picture of energies of this year and given that it is all moving toward our collective transitioning into an "age of Aquarius."

So on this day, we invite you to delve into your quiet, new moon self, to settle into the deep and the quiet and to listen to the deepest, most inner voice that will come through when you are still and quiet inside yourself. What does it need to say? What intentions are you naturally ready to set? Let go of any ideas of what you "should" say or "should" intend in this moment. In particular, we invite you to feel into the energies around Aquarius. What intentions might bubble up from your deep, quiet self regarding your innovative, unique voice that is maybe from the future, from the cosmos, from the unknown and the infinity of possibilities? What intention does your soul want to set that might have to do with your sense of collective good or friendships or working in groups for the good of our future? Listen deeply and simply be in this still, new moment.

The Cosmic Flow Through You

In this deep, still, dark, quiet moment of this new moon, I listen deeply inside myself and to the collective dark all around me. I feel the dark moon sitting next to the sun and surrounded by the stars. It has a quiet message. There is a quiet, still message inside me. What is coming through in this moment is....

SATURDAY, FEBRUARY 8, 2020

Full Moon in Leo, 20 degrees, 00', 11:33pm, PST

Getting Centered in You

We invite you to start by taking a deep breath, dropping into your true center, your beautiful and pure soul. And from this place, name what is true for you...

Today, I am feeling...

In this moment, what is present for me is...

Today, I am needing...

Today, mine to do is...

Our Message for You

Today is a full moon in Leo. This is a beautiful energy. The full light of the sun (which rules Leo) is shining its light on the moon which is sitting in front of the constellation and energies of Leo.

As we stated above, Leo is ruled by the Sun. Leo is the king, the queen, the lion, the lioness. Leo is on the stage and loves to be the center of attention. Leo needs to be witnessed and praised. Leo has a big heart and loves to shine and to be seen in that shining way. Leo is creative and relates to all that we create, including our children. Leo can be very loving and also somewhat self centered at times. Leo is expression of all kinds in warm and wonderful ways that need to be seen and need to be shared in our world.

Think back to the intentions and energies that you felt on the last new moon on January 24, 2020. Feel into how those intentions may have played out over the past two weeks and how they may have come to fruition or may be having a light shone on them now.

And in general, feel into what energies are needing and wanting to be highlighted at this time. In particular, what aspects of your creativity in the world or the creative forces around you may need to shine through or have extra attention?

The Cosmic Flow Through You

Today, on this full moon in Leo, I close my eyes and see my shining, beautiful, seen self. The parts of me that need to shine, that need to be seen are…

Today, I have an opportunity to notice what parts of me are having the chance to be seen, to be praised, to be loved out in the open and to notice which parts of myself might need or want to come more fully out onto the stage. My full, openly expressed self says…..

My full, openly expressed self does…..

I let go of all stage fright, of any hiding behind any curtains and come out fully as…

My intentions from two weeks ago on the New Moon were….

Today, I notice that the energies of those intentions have moved in these ways….

I deserve to be seen, to be praised, to be loved and known in all of who I am. This reality feels like….

My creativity goes on and on and on. It can be expressed in these ways and so many more….

I give so much gratitude today for….

SUNDAY, FEBRUARY 16, 2020

Mercury Goes Retrograde at 12 degrees Pisces

Getting Centered in You

We invite you to start by taking a deep breath, dropping into your true center, your beautiful and pure soul. And from this place, name what is true for you...

Today, I am feeling...

In this moment, what is present for me is...

Today, I am needing...

Today, mine to do is...

Our Message for You

Mercury Retrograde can be a funny time. It has the reputation of causing many "issues" and problems with communication and technology. This can be true. One association with the energy of something going "retrograde" can be that it is doing the "wrong" thing. However, the energy of something "retrograding" is also that it is backing up and giving us a chance to reflect, to review, to do something again in a new and different, more evolved way.

So in this moment of Mercury going retrograde in the sign of Pisces and then into Aquarius until March 9, 2020, we invite you, rather than getting scared of what might "go wrong" in this period of time, we invite you to sit with this opportunity to reflect on what you may be revisiting or what you have an opportunity to re-make, re-create, do over again in a new, more practiced and conscious way. The energy of Mercury going back through the first degrees of Pisces and then dipping into the late degrees of Aquarius, can give us a chance to revisit our relationship and our thoughts and stories regarding our relationship to the All That Is, the collective, the chaos of all of existence, the beauty of all of existence, the mysterious, the magical, the intuitive, and so forth.

We invite you on this day and over the next three weeks as Mercury is "revisiting" the first part of Pisces and the end of Aquarius to simply sink into the ride. Mercury is revisiting a beautiful set of energies that can be highly poetic, highly musical and resonant. And mercury going retrograde can provide an extra boost of communicating in these ways with an extra flair, a unique bent that no one has ever done before. So embrace that chance. Have fun. See where the cosmos wants to take you and just sing and dance along.

The Cosmic Flow Through You

In this moment when Mercury is retracing its steps back through the sign of Pisces and then into Aquarius, I sink into this ride through the cosmos, through the music and songs and beauty of the All That Is. In this moment, I feel, I hear, and I see…

Over the course of this retrograde period from February 16, 2020 to March 9, 2020, I notice, I observe, I feel, I sing….

SUNDAY, FEBRUARY 23, 2020

New Moon in Pisces, 4 degrees, 28', 7:31am, PST

Getting Centered in You

We invite you to start by taking a deep breath, dropping into your true center, your beautiful and pure soul. And from this place, name what is true for you...

Today, I am feeling...

In this moment, what is present for me is...

Today, I am needing...

Today, mine to do is...

Our Message for You

Today there is a new moon in Pisces. This means that the moon and sun are sitting together in the energies of Pisces and there is a chance to start fresh - yet again - and this time in particular in the energies of Pisces.

As stated above, Pisces is ruled by the planet Neptune and historically by Jupiter. Pisces is the sign of the All that Is. Pisces is ether and the chaos and all knowingness of everything. Pisces is all of existence. Pisces is our intuition, our knowing and divinity and purest love through our hearts. Pisces is the ethereal. Pisces can be related to addiction and depression and despondency. Pisces can help us to channel what needs to come through from all of existence, the spirit world, and the energies of all things. Pisces is beautiful in its own divine way and reminds us that we are all truly one.

The Cosmic Flow Through You

On this new moon in Pisces, I feel into the energies of the beautiful, infinite All That Is, the mysteries of existence, the ethereal and the oneness of all. I listen to those energies inside myself and I hear and feel a new intention which is….

I close my eyes, feel into the beautiful moon sitting in quiet stillness today and she flows through me...

Full Moon in Virgo, 19 degrees, 36', 10:47am, PST

Mercury Goes Direct at 28 Degrees Aquarius

Getting Centered in You

We invite you to start by taking a deep breath, dropping into your true center, your beautiful and pure soul. And from this place, name what is true for you...

Today, I am feeling...

In this moment, what is present for me is...

Today, I am needing...

Today, mine to do is...

Our Message for You

Today is a full moon in the beautiful sign of Virgo. Virgo is ruled by Mercury, just like Gemini. Virgo is beautiful. Virgo is discriminating. Virgo can be a true healer. Virgo is down to earth and practical. Virgo is diligent and works hard. Virgo is persistent and methodical. Virgo is self contained and perceptive. Virgo is clean and clears out what is no longer needed. Virgo is reliable and true. Interestingly, Mercury (the ruler of Virgo) also goes direct today at 28 degrees of Aquarius.

So today we invite you to do three things today:

1) Sink into the energies of Virgo and the fullness of the Virgo energies in you and what might want or need to be expressed on this full moon.

2) Think back to the new moon two weeks ago on February 23, 2020. Review your intentions on that day and observe and reflect on how the energies of those intentions have moved or shifted or come to fruition as of now.

3) Review the period of the last three weeks of Mercury in retrograde since February 16, 2020. Look back at what came through for you on that day and reflect on what your soul may have been reviewing or "re-doing" as Mercury has journeyed back through Pisces and the last two degrees of Aquarius.

The Cosmic Flow Through You

On this full moon in Virgo, I close my eyes and allow myself to be enveloped with the energies of clean beauty, discrimination, hard work, persistence, and healing. I allow Virgo to show and move through me whatever I am needing to bring through to fully shine and manifest on this full moon. The energies of fullness in Virgo say....

On the new moon in Pisces two weeks ago, my intentions were....

I think back over the past two weeks and notice....

In addition, over the past three weeks, Mercury has been slowly sailing backward through the first half of Pisces and into the end degrees of Aquarius. As Mercury stations and begins to move direct again today, I feel myself having learned and reviewed…..

As Mercury stations direct at 28 degrees Aquarius, he assists me to pick up an important energy of the end of the Aquarius sign and then to again move through my ability to think and communicate and receive communication through the energies of the ethereal Pisces. In this moment of stationing direct and beginning to move forward again, Mercury says through me….

SATURDAY, MARCH 21, 2020

Saturn Enters Aquarius

Getting Centered in You

We invite you to start by taking a deep breath, dropping into your true center, your beautiful and pure soul. And from this place, name what is true for you...

Today, I am feeling...

In this moment, what is present for me is...

Today, I am needing...

Today, mine to do is...

Our Message for You

Today, Saturn enters Aquarius until July 1, 2020. It will journey forward and dip into Aquarius until July 1, 2020 when it re-enters Capricorn to help us review our lessons of Capricorn once again until it finally moves into Aquarius for real on December 17, 2020. This temporary sojourn of Saturn into Aquarius for the next three months and a bit gives us a chance to get a taste of what it feels like to have the elder teacher of Saturn move from the sign of "the way things have been" (Capricorn) into the sign of the future (Aquarius). This gives us a boost in our ability to envision and try out new ways of structuring our inner worlds and our societies. What visions come up for you today and in this entire stretch of weeks? What does this time ignite in you? Pay attention to your dreams, to what bolts of lightening you might feel in your body or in your thoughts regarding new ways of doing things, new ways of organizing yourself, your life, your groups, your communities, our entire world. We invite you to tap into your own elder teacher self, your wise one who is a visionary of the future - literally - and who has the ability to begin to construct the new reality that you see.

The Cosmic Flow Through You

On this day when Saturn enters Aquarius for a period of just over three months, I tap into this elder teacher friend who is Saturn. I tap into this part of myself as well and I move into my ability and my gift to en-vision our future, our new structures inside ourselves and in our communities and in our world. The energy of the grand teacher elder visionary says through me....

TUESDAY, MARCH 24, 2020

NEW MOON IN ARIES, 4 degrees, 12', 2:28am, PST

Getting Centered in You

We invite you to start by taking a deep breath, dropping into your true center, your beautiful and pure soul. And from this place, name what is true for you...

Today, I am feeling...

In this moment, what is present for me is...

Today, I am needing...

Today, mine to do is...

Our Message for You

Today there is a new moon in Aries. Aries is ruled by the planet Mars. Aries is the warrior, the god of war. Aries is fire and "go get 'em" nature. Aries is drive and instinct. Aries charges ahead and penetrates. Aries is a spark that kicks you out of bed and says, "On with it!" Aries gets things started and can catalyze change.

On this new moon in Aries, we invite you to sink into the dark of your inner self and to connect to your inner fire, your inner warrior, your spark to initiate, to drive, to move, to claim your BEINGness. You exist. You are here. You are present. We invite you to claim this fact. We invite you to fully claim that you ARE here. All of your spirit, your being, your soul, your self IS here, right here, right now. This is the Aries energy saying, "YES. I exist. I am. Let's go!"

The Cosmic Flow Through You

On this new moon in Aries, I take a deep breath. I close my eyes and feel into the spark inside myself until I click with that spark. I hear a voice that smiles and says, "I am here. I matter. ALL of me matters. ALL of me is present and IS." I breathe into this spark and smile and let it speak. The spark of beingness and fire in me says....

As I feel into this spark in me, I feel the following intentions ignite and move through me....

SATURDAY, APRIL 4, 2020

JUPITER AND PLUTO CONJUNCTION
24 degrees Capricorn

Getting Centered in You

We invite you to start by taking a deep breath, dropping into your true center, your beautiful and pure soul. And from this place, name what is true for you...

Today, I am feeling...

In this moment, what is present for me is...

Today, I am needing...

Today, mine to do is...

Our Message for You

Today is the first of three conjunctions between Jupiter and Pluto in Capricorn in 2020. This conjunction holds an energy of Jupiter, the biggest of the planets in your solar system, connecting with the energy of Pluto, the planet of our deep soul, power, and transformation. They are coming together in the sign of Capricorn which is the sign that pertains to many things, including the structures within ourselves and in our greater world.

Therefore, one way to think of this conjunction is that it holds the potential to be akin to a wrecking ball that hits our deepest seated notions about power and our internal and societal structures. This might manifest in many ways, some of which could feel difficult or could feel liberating and freeing. We would like to encourage you to essentially stay conscious and aware and if you have a sense of a "wrecking ball" hitting aspects of your life, either subtly or not so subtly, take this as an opportunity to "get behind" the energy of that destructive force. Notice what it is targeting, what it is tearing down, what parts of yourself or your world are being asked or forced to die, to deconstruct, to transform.

As you potentially feel this force in your life or observe it in the world, we invite you to feel into what the wisdom is in this destruction. What does it want to say? What is it making room for? What does the crashing structure feel like? What does the empty space left feel like behind in the place of the structure that has come down? How does your soul see that space taking shape in the ways that are new and fresh and ready to come into existence? What does this new space feel like, look like, taste like, act like? Take a moment to go deeply into these energies, flow with any difficult times you might be experiencing, and open up to the new possibilities that are being shown and that are ready to be created through you.

Over the year, as Jupiter retrogrades and then comes back to conjunct Pluto two more times, this potential for destruction and then envisioning and re-creation will come in waves. This is simply the first of those three waves. So be gentle, be easy on yourself. Today and this moment are simply about being with the feelings, being with the energies of what could be, what was, what is the purest version of what could be to come.

The Cosmic Flow Through You

In this moment, I sit with the knowing that our world is about to change. It is changing. I feel a stirring in me. I know that as things fall down, new things have the opportunity to arise. I close my eyes and feel deeply into what, if anything, I feel falling down, being destroyed, dying inside myself and in the world. I take a moment to feel and notice this destruction. What I see and feel and hear and know is.....

As I feel the destruction and aspects of my internal or external structures crashing, I also feel the empty space that this destruction is creating. This empty space feels like……

I take a deep breath and feel into the destruction and the empty space and I know that I am on this planet to help to create a new way, a new world, a new way for us all of being in the world. I tune into my own, truest, most pure soul and the collective divine and I am shown…..

Today, as I sit with all of these feelings, I know and am reminded that everything is ok. I am given a reminder of…

I anchor into the Light and know that even if destruction occurs in any area of my life, I can remain connected to my anchor(s) of…..

I take deep breaths, move with grace, and know that I am here right here right now by choice and that this is all part of my own plan in concert with the divine.

TUESDAY, APRIL 7, 2020

FULL MOON IN LIBRA, 18 degrees, 7:34pm, PST

Getting Centered in You

We invite you to start by taking a deep breath, dropping into your true center, your beautiful and pure soul. And from this place, name what is true for you...

Today, I am feeling...

In this moment, what is present for me is...

Today, I am needing...

Today, mine to do is...

Our Message for You

Today is a full moon in Libra, the beautiful sign of the scales, of balance, of harmony. Libra is ruled by Venus. Libra is a kind of beauty, slightly different in quality from earthy, beautiful Virgo. Libra is balanced and in tune with "the other." Libra is the sign related to partnerships of all kinds, of working and balancing with the others, including in marriage partnerships. Libra likes harmony and can be co-dependent. Libra often needs to balance with its polarity of Aries to learn to be independent while also interdependent. Libra is a wonderful listener and can truly understand all sides of a situation. Libra is a great mediator and friend.

The Cosmic Flow Through You

On this day of the full moon in Libra, I feel into the energies of harmony and beauty and justice inside of me. I notice what aspects of these energies are needing to come to light, to be shone on, to come into full fruition. I take a deep breath and feel, hear, see.....

On this day, I also think back to the new moon two weeks ago on March 24, 2020. On that day, when the new moon was in Aries, I set the following intentions….

As I feel into the intentions I set on the new moon two weeks ago, I notice and feel…..

The energies of Libra need to say today….

I tune into the big, beautiful, full moon today and she says….

Moving forward, I carry with me….

WEDNESDAY, APRIL 22, 2020

NEW MOON IN TAURUS, 3 degrees, 7:25pm, PST

Getting Centered in You

We invite you to start by taking a deep breath, dropping into your true center, your beautiful and pure soul. And from this place, name what is true for you...

Today, I am feeling...

In this moment, what is present for me is...

Today, I am needing...

Today, mine to do is...

Our Message for You

Today, there is a new moon in Taurus. The sun and the moon conjunct in a fresh cycle in the energy of Taurus. Taurus is ruled by the planet Venus. Taurus is "the bull." Taurus is the grounded, sensual nature of home and clothing and textures. Taurus likes being fixed and earthy. Taurus loves to curl up with a book and stay cozy in a warm bed. Taurus is sensual and sexual in the physical world. Taurus loves beautiful things and loves to be held and touched. Taurus loves a good massage and the smell of gorgeous flowers and the sun on the skin. Taurus is steady and true.

On this day of this new moon in Taurus, we have the opportunity to set new intentions, to feel into the groundedness, the beauty, the steadfast and loyal aspects of ourselves. We have the opportunity to feel into the parts of ourselves that may be needing to get in touch with our own self value, our own self worth, to voice, even to ourselves, what we are truly desiring, feeling, needing, in our physical world, in our sense of comfort and beauty and worthiness in ourselves.

The Cosmic Flow Through You

Today on this new moon in Taurus, I drop into the dark center of myself, of my soul. I feel into what spark of new, true energy and aliveness is speaking in me today. I feel into what needs or wants to birth into the world today as the spirit world sets an intention for me and through me at the beginning of this new cycle between our moon and our sun. I take a deep breath, breathe out slowly and feel this intention setting through.

The intention(s) that emerge are....

Today I feel into the energies of the sign of Taurus. I feel into my sense of beauty and sensuousness, my physical sexuality, my need for touch, my need to be held and known, my need to value myself, my enjoyment of my physical senses and of the world. I feel into my own ability to be loyal and steady, calm and even. I feel into my desire for quiet and time alone, my desire to retreat into my own world and be cozy and contained comfortably within myself or maybe with one other. I take a deep breath and notice what these energies in and moving through me need or want to say. Perhaps they move or dance or sing. Perhaps they simply have a language of touch or they make a sound. I feel into whatever this is for me right here right now and what I notice is....

I am loved, I am held, I am valuable. In fact, I am so valuable, I am literally made of the same substance as the stars. I am infinite value. I am perfection, just exactly as I am. I can sit in this way of being and self value and simply BE.

SATURDAY, APRIL 25, 2020

PLUTO GOES RETROGRADE
24 degrees Capricorn

Getting Centered in You

We invite you to start by taking a deep breath, dropping into your true center, your beautiful and pure soul. And from this place, name what is true for you...

Today, I am feeling...

In this moment, what is present for me is...

Today, I am needing...

Today, mine to do is...

Our Message for You

Today, Pluto goes retrograde at 24 degrees Capricorn. It will be going retrograde very slowly until it turns direct again in just over five months on October 4, 2020 at 22 degrees Capricorn.

The powerful planet of Pluto represents our deepest soul, deep and radical transformation, death, the taboo, and so forth. Pluto going retrograde in Capricorn gives us a pause, a moment to go deeper, to feel into our individual and collective souls to feel into exactly what we are being called to transform, to allow to die, to allow to change and evolve radically, right here and right now.

The Cosmic Flow Through You

On this day as Pluto goes retrograde in Capricorn and as he rides retrograde over the next five and a half months, I sink into my underworld, deepest soul. In this place of dark, deep, radical transformation, I feel and see and know....

The energies I feel my soul reviewing and revisiting are....

I affirm that radical transformation is ok and that I am safe and can let go and let the transformations happen gracefully and allow the things that need to die to go and the things that are right to come in to flow in right and perfect timing.

WEDNESDAY, MAY 6, 2020

NORTH NODE OF THE MOON ENTERS GEMINI
SOUTH NODE ENTERS SAGITTARIUS

Getting Centered in You

We invite you to start by taking a deep breath, dropping into your true center, your beautiful and pure soul. And from this place, name what is true for you...

Today, I am feeling...

In this moment, what is present for me is...

Today, I am needing...

Today, mine to do is...

Our Message for You

Today, the nodes of the moon switch from being in Capricorn and Cancer to being in Sagittarius and Gemini. The nodes will stay in these signs until January 18, 2022. This is a major shift in energy for the collective as a whole and for you each individually. This shift indicates many things, but brings a beautiful and not coincidental opportunity given the shifts in energy this year. Over the past year and a half of the nodes being in Capricorn and Cancer, the collective soul intention was around balance of the past energies in Capricorn (structure, top-down authority, getting things done, how things "should" be, etc.) with the energies of Cancer (our inner child, most vulnerable selves, our need to be held and nurtured, etc.). Now the collective soul intention has moved into the balance between Gemini and Sagittarius. This provides a beautiful opportunity. The north node is in Gemini which means that we are being pulled and supported into the energies of learning, curiosity, newness, fresh knowledge, quick thinking communication, speaking, teaching in ways that many can understand, writing, and so forth. We are bringing through our past energies of Sagittarius (with the south node being in Sagittarius now). Sagittarius involves energies of the guru, the teacher on a bigger scale, belief systems, higher education, the broad world, and so forth.

The energies of Gemini are a beautiful addition to this shift we are making into the collective transition from the energies of Capricorn into the age of Aquarius. Gemini allows us to come into this time with a sense of being a beginner learner, a sense that we don't know all there is to know and that we are all in this together. It also provides energy for communicating, for speaking, for talking and dialoguing with each other, for writing and sharing our thoughts and learning about where we are wanting to take our world next.

Today we invite you to simply feel into these energies of Gemini, in particular, but also of Sagittarius - of the parts of you that are the guru teacher, the speaker, the writer, the communicator, the learner, the curious one, the one who does not know and is open and eager to take in life in a new way.

The Cosmic Flow Through You

Today as I feel the south node of the moon enter Sagittarius and the north node of the moon enter Gemini, I sink into the parts of myself that have been the wise sage, the guru teacher, the traveler, the citizen of the big world. These are my energies of Sagittarius. As I feel into this energy of the current south node of the moon, I feel....

I now feel into the energies of Gemini - the parts of me that are the learner, the one who is curious about many things, about life, who is open to new possibilities, new information, and who is a communicator - a writer, speaker, a person who is sharing in dialogue with others. As I take a deep breath and breathe into this energy of where the north node of the moon now sits, I feel...

Sagittarius is bringing in....

Gemini is opening me and all of us to.....

THURSDAY, MAY 7, 2020

FULL MOON IN SCORPIO, 17 degrees, 3:45am, PST

Getting Centered in You

We invite you to start by taking a deep breath, dropping into your true center, your beautiful and pure soul. And from this place, name what is true for you...

Today, I am feeling...

In this moment, what is present for me is...

Today, I am needing...

Today, mine to do is...

Our Message for You

Today the moon is full in the sign of Scorpio. Scorpio is ruled by the planet Pluto and historically ruled by Mars. Scorpio is deep and dark. Scorpio is related to the underworld, the areas of depth and death that people often are afraid of. Scorpio is incredibly perceptive and likes to bring up and talk about things that often get left unsaid or unnamed. Scorpio is the taboo. Scorpio is death. Scorpio is the deep healer, the medicine man and medicine woman, the sage, the elder of the deep, the shaman. Scorpio has a deep magic and incredible power. Scorpio helps things to die over and over and over again and is crucial in assisting us to let go of anything that is no longer serving the deepest, most true evolution of our soul.

The Cosmic Flow Through You

Today on this day of a full moon in Scorpio, I feel into the energies of deep, dark soul - the parts of me that can feel the depths of all of reality - the taboo, the merging, the sexual, the painful, the death, the endings, the transformations that must happen. Today the sun is shining a light on this deep, possibly hidden part of myself. And as the sun shines this light on this deep part of myself, I feel this deep soul in me saying….

Today I feel the moon herself and she comes to me and says….

I also think back two weeks to the last new moon which was on April 22, 2020. The intentions I set then were…

I feel into and observe the energies of those intentions that I set on that new moon two weeks ago and I notice, I feel….

SUNDAY, MAY 10, 2020

SATURN TURNS RETROGRADE at 1 degree Aquarius

Getting Centered in You

We invite you to start by taking a deep breath, dropping into your true center, your beautiful and pure soul. And from this place, name what is true for you...

Today, I am feeling...

In this moment, what is present for me is...

Today, I am needing...

Today, mine to do is...

Our Message for You

Today, Saturn has dipped its toe into Aquarius since March 21, 2020. It is now at 1 degree Aquarius and is going retrograde to head back into Capricorn, its own sign.

One way to think of this little dip of Saturn into Aquarius is that he has tested the "air" of Aquarius and has given us a little taste of his energy in Aquarius and now he is heading back into Capricorn to let us settle more deeply into whatever lessons or support we might need from his energy in Capricorn before he heads forward again and back into Aquarius for real on December 17, 2020 and then conjuncts Jupiter at 0 degrees Aquarius on December 21, 2020 - the big day of "hallelujah."

Saturn will be going backward in the beginning degree of Aquarius from today until July 1, 2020 when it will re-enter Capricorn. So on this day that Saturn is at 1 degree Aquarius and is turning to head back toward Capricorn, we encourage you to use today and the next few weeks until July 1, 2020 to feel into what this revisiting of this "dip" into Aquarius feels like for you.

As we stated above, Saturn in Aquarius is an energy of allowing ourselves to re-vision and re-create our sense of structures, both internally and in our societies, in new, innovative, creative, out of the box ways. This is an energy that opens our minds and our visions to what the stars may want to say, what our collective souls may want to say to and through us about how we can possibly re-create the structures of our world and of our consciousness and our approach to everything and anything in an infinite number of ways.

So this is a time that calls us to be the wise elder visionaries as Saturn heads back toward Capricorn to then pick up some deeper wisdom about how the "how" of those visions can come into manifestations.

So for now, let your vision open. Let your wise self fly in the cosmos and just see what it sees.

The Cosmic Flow Through You

On this day that Saturn is turning retrograde at 1 degree Aquarius and taking a slow sojourn back to Capricorn between now and July 1, 2020, I sink into my wise, elder visionary self. I take a deep breath and open my third eye, open any and all of me and my access to the collective unconscious and whatever visions are meant to open through me. I close my eyes and I see....

The structures in me that I feel changing are.....

The structures in my world that I feel changing are....

The cosmos is calling me to.....

Mine to do next is.....

WEDNESDAY, MAY 13, 2020

VENUS GOES RETROGRADE at 22 degrees Gemini
(Until June 26, 2020 when it goes direct at 6 degrees Gemini)

Getting Centered in You

We invite you to start by taking a deep breath, dropping into your true center, your beautiful and pure soul. And from this place, name what is true for you...

Today, I am feeling...

In this moment, what is present for me is...

Today, I am needing...

Today, mine to do is...

Our Message for You

Today, Venus goes retrograde at 22 degrees Gemini. Venus goes retrograde typically about every 18 months or so, so not all that often.

Venus going retrograde, just like any other planet going retrograde, allows us to re-visit, re-vision, re-do that area of our lives, our selves, our consciousness.

In the case of Venus going retrograde in Gemini, this is a time when we can re-view and re-visit areas of our lives and ourselves that are reflected in the energies of Venus - those regarding love, beauty, money, relationships, self-value, and so forth. In particular, given that this retrograde is in Gemini, this can be a good time to re-visit and re-vise and re-do our self-talk, our communication with others, our sense of connecting to ourselves and others through words, through speech, even through music and song. This is a time when we may be able to see more clearly how we are communicating to ourselves, what we tell ourselves in narratives in our minds and hearts and bodies.

So during this day and in the Venus retrograde period of the next 43 days, we invite you to sink into this notion of reviewing, revising, and re-visiting your own relationship to what it means to speak kindly, speak harshly, communicate love and beauty and all kinds of self talk and talk between yourself and others you truly care about. This is just one aspect of the energies of Venus going retrograde in Gemini, but this is the one that we are most focused on today and that we are highlighting. We encourage you to take time to dive deep. Venus is a sensitive planet, a sensitive set of energies inside of you. Be gentle, be kind, be giving and loving with yourself and just see what you see, see what you feel, notice what you need and give it to yourself.

The Cosmic Flow Through You

During this day and over the period of 43 days coming up while Venus is going retrograde in Gemini, I sink into the part of myself that loves, that IS love, that is beauty, that is value. I sink into the part of myself that communicates love to myself, to others, to the world. I sink into the part of me that values myself and my home, that is receptive and feels surrounded by love. I feel into the part of myself that knows that I need, that knows what I hold to be true and right for myself. I feel into what I need to say to myself, what I need to say to others and what comes through is....

THURSDAY, MAY 14, 2020

JUPITER GOES RETROGRADE at 27 degrees
Capricorn

Getting Centered in You

We invite you to start by taking a deep breath, dropping into your true center, your beautiful and pure soul. And from this place, name what is true for you...

Today, I am feeling...

In this moment, what is present for me is...

Today, I am needing...

Today, mine to do is...

Our Message for You

Today, one day after Venus goes retrograde in Gemini, Capricorn goes retrograde in Capricorn. These energies of retrograde give us a double feeling of retracing our steps, of being able to double our efforts and our energies in reviewing our values, as well as our commitment to our work and our determination to re-vision and re-create the structures within ourselves and our world. What a perfect pair. These energies give us an opportunity to way to include our sense of love and values in how we hope to rebuild our world. This is a beautiful time. Do not be scared of the retrogrades. Go with them. Embrace them. Imagine that you are on a raft in a river and are being pulled backward, against the current of the stream and you have the chance to see again the view that you may have only partially seen as you came down this river the first time. Just take a deep breath and enjoy the ride. And while you are enjoying the ride and viewing the bank, start to notice what you feel in this reviewing time. What comes to you differently or in a new way, especially regarding the energies that you felt on or near April 4, 2020 when Jupiter first was conjunct Pluto at 24 degrees Capricorn? Jupiter is now heading back toward Pluto and will conjunct Pluto for the second time this year on June 30, 2020. Take this time to reflect, feel, take in the sights that you may have missed.

The Cosmic Flow Through You

Today as Jupiter goes retrograde at 27 degrees Capricorn, I take a deep breath and feel into these energies of Capricorn that are the river and river bank that Jupiter is riding down. I remember what was coming through for me on April 4, 2020 when Jupiter conjuncted Pluto at 24 degrees Capricorn. I take a deep breath and feel into what this ride with Jupiter is reviewing for me. What comes through is….

FRIDAY, MAY 22, 2020

NEW MOON IN GEMINI, 2 degrees, 10:38am, PST

Getting Centered in You

We invite you to start by taking a deep breath, dropping into your true center, your beautiful and pure soul. And from this place, name what is true for you...

Today, I am feeling...

In this moment, what is present for me is...

Today, I am needing...

Today, mine to do is...

Our Message for You

Today is a new moon in Gemini. As we have said above, Gemini lends some wonderful energies to this time. Gemini is ruled by the planet Mercury. Gemini is a communicator. Gemini loves to talk and think and speak and write and say whatever is on its mind. Gemini loves to learn and has to do with childhood, siblings, and primary school. Gemini can think fast, is an air sign, and can be flighty, moving from thing to thing to thing to thing. Gemini is often curious and inquisitive. Gemini can be dualistic and secretive. Gemini can also be a great explainer of details and important information. Gemini is a great energy for helping the world to understand many things better.

At this new moon in Gemini, we encourage you to, yet again, feel into these energies of Gemini where the north node of the moon also resides, currently in the end degrees of the sign. Feel deep into your quiet self, the part of you that is calling to start a new, fresh cycle. What is calling to you to start new in yourself or in your life? Take a deep breath, get very still and quiet and listen deep.

The Cosmic Flow Through You

Today, at this new moon in Gemini, I feel into the quiet, still energy of the moon which is currently conjunct with its companion, the sun. I take a deep breath and sink deep deep deep into myself. I go deep until I feel completely still and quiet and I click with that new spark in myself. I listen to the quiet of the moon and the quiet of myself and I hear and feel what needs to come through and what intentions need to come through me for this time moving forward. What comes through is....

FRIDAY, JUNE 5, 2020

FULL MOON IN SAGITTARIUS,
15 degrees, 12:12pm, PST

LUNAR ECLIPSE,
15 degrees Gemini, 12:26pm, PST
(Sun at 15 degrees Gemini and Venus nearly conjunct the Sun at 12 degrees Gemini)

Getting Centered in You

We invite you to start by taking a deep breath, dropping into your true center, your beautiful and pure soul. And from this place, name what is true for you...

Today, I am feeling...

In this moment, what is present for me is...

Today, I am needing...

Today, mine to do is...

Our Message for You

On this day of the full moon in Sagittarius, there is also a powerful and beautiful first eclipse on the Sagittarius-Gemini axis. This is the first time in many years that the eclipse energy has been a portal essentially for us to bring through and initiate the energies of the new universal nodes of the moon in Sagittarius and Gemini. A beautiful aspect of this particular eclipse is that Venus is nearly conjunct the sun in Gemini, still going retrograde. So this eclipse gives us an opportunity to channel, to bring through from the energy of the full moon in Sagittarius near the south node of the moon into the energies of the the north node of the moon nearby the sun and Venus in Gemini. What a beautiful set of energies to feel into.

We encourage you to understand and know these energies in whatever way is right for you. However, we would like to highlight that one way of experiencing these energies is that the sun is shining full onto the moon in Sagittarius who knows our personal, deep connection to our Sagittarius selves - our past as guru teachers, world travelers, adventurers, intuitive scholars of belief and great wisdom of many kinds. This light of this full moon is then channeled back through the portal of this eclipse to balance with its counterpart of the sun and Venus in Gemini. The fullness of the moon in Sagittarius is, in a sense, filling up the sun and Venus in Gemini, giving us a chance to remember our big wisdom regarding many things and then to bring that into our smaller worlds, our worlds of our inner values, our selves who are fresh learners, our ability to be curious in the world, curious with each other, curious in love, curious in loving ourselves and loving each other.

Our teacher guru selves can support us in coming to our relationships and our communication with ourselves and with each other in a deep, yet new way that is confident and yet humble at the same time.

The Cosmic Flow Through You

On this day of the full moon in Sagittarius and an eclipse in the Gemini-Sagittarius axis, I fall deeply into the energies of this beautiful, swirling changes that are happening in me and in the world. I feel into the love. I feel into me as guru. I feel into me as world traveller, scholar, adventurer of great things. I feel this part of me fall through the portal of the eclipse and land squarely in my sense of love and being loved, of being seen and known and of communicating in confident and yet humble ways with myself and with others. I take a deep breath and feel how and where these energies need to take me. I go with them and I am taken....

In these energies, I am shown....

In these energies, I hear....

In this eclipse, I am transformed....

THURSDAY, JUNE 18, 2020

MERCURY GOES RETROGRADE
14 degrees Cancer

Getting Centered in You

We invite you to start by taking a deep breath, dropping into your true center, your beautiful and pure soul. And from this place, name what is true for you...

Today, I am feeling...

In this moment, what is present for me is...

Today, I am needing...

Today, mine to do is...

Our Message for You

Today is the beginning of the second mercury retrograde this year. As we mentioned at the beginning of the first mercury retrograde earlier this year, Mercury Retrograde can be a funny time. It often has the reputation of causing many "issues" and problems with communication and technology. This certainly can be true. One association with the energy of something going "retrograde" can be that it is going "backward" or doing the wrong thing. However, the energy of something "retrograding" is also that it is going "backward" in the sense that it is backing up and giving us a chance to reflect, to review, to do something again in a new and different, more evolved way.

The first time this year that Mercury went retrograde was in the signs of Pisces and Aquarius. This time, it is going retrograde at 14 degrees Cancer and will station direct on July 12, 2020, at 5 degrees Cancer. So in this mercury retrograde, we have an opportunity to review and re-do the energies of Cancer - our relationship to our inner, most vulnerable selves.

As we stated above, Cancer is ruled by the Moon. Similar to the moon, cancer is often sweet and sensitive. Cancer is the sign of the mother and childhood. Cancer is the most vulnerable and inner part of oneself. Cancer is the most raw, truth of who we are deep down, the part of us that needs to be treated tenderly and with honor and great care. Cancer can be watery and emotional, with ups and downs changing in rapid pace. Cancer has great wisdom in what we truly need and can speak purely if we listen with great quiet.

So let's take a chance to go deep, go into the cocoon of who we are, deep down, tender and sweet and held inside ourselves. During this period of just over three weeks, take this opportunity to come into this place inside yourself. Who are you in the most raw, vulnerable part of you? What are you truly feeling? What are you truly needing? What does your inner child and inner most self need or want to say? What needs nurturing in you and in your world?

The Cosmic Flow Through You

On this day when Mercury goes retrograde in Cancer, I drop into the inner most part of my vulnerable, raw self. In here, I feel…

In my inner, most raw and vulnerable self, I hear….

My inner, raw and vulnerable self says....

I hold myself by....

I feel at home inside myself. I am surrounded by love and care in myself. I hold myself and feel held by the womb of the world. I am rocked by the arms of the divine and by the sway of the cosmos. And all is well.

SATURDAY, JUNE 20, 2020
SUMMER SOLSTICE

NEW MOON IN CANCER, 0 degrees, 11:41pm, PST

ANNULAR SOLAR ECLIPSE, 0 degrees Cancer, 11:41pm, PST

(North Node is nearly conjunct the sun and moon one degree away at 29 degrees Gemini)

Getting Centered in You

We invite you to start by taking a deep breath, dropping into your true center, your beautiful and pure soul. And from this place, name what is true for you...

Today, I am feeling...

In this moment, what is present for me is...

Today, I am needing...

Today, mine to do is...

Our Message for You

Happy Summer and Winter Solstice (depending on your hemisphere!)....

Today is quite a magical day.... It is the summer solstice and also both a new moon and solar eclipse at 0 degrees Cancer. The north node of the moon is one degree away from the sun at 29 degrees of Gemini.

This longest day of the year in the northern hemisphere and shortest day of the day in the year in the Southern Hemisphere lends an extra magic and an extra "thinning of the veils" today.

Today as the energies move through the portal of this eclipse, we are particularly feeling the opportunity for you to bring through your ability to communicate in new ways - again - your deepest, most vulnerable and truest, raw self. This is a theme we are seeing over and over again in the rhythms of this year. Getting in touch with your most raw and vulnerable self and finding ways to communicate those realities are key to the transformation of your and our world. This is a key to healing, to true healing within ourselves, in individual relationships, and in the world at large. That is why these energies are providing you this opportunity over and over again.

This is beautiful.... ride with it. See where it goes, what needs to be heard.

By the end of this year, you will be an expert at hearing, loving, and cradling your own vulnerable self. And hopefully you will have devised and developed some beautiful new ways of moving in relationship to your communication of this part of yourself both within yourself and with others.

On this day of gratitude, of a celebration of the dance of the trio of the sun, the moon, and the earth, we invite you to first simply take a moment to revel in the beauty of this world, of the sun itself, of the moon herself, of the Earth herself. Take a moment to feel how the three of these beautiful creatures do a perpetual dance with each other and how they are in constant, true, perfect balance with each other. What do you feel in this balance, in this dance? Where is your dance with them? Ride with it. You are part of it - literally. You are part of them - again, literally.

The Cosmic Flow Through You

On this day of the summer solstice, the new moon in Cancer, and the solar eclipse, I sink into the beauty and celebration of the sun, of the moon, of this Earth, and of the dance that they are doing with each other all the time and that I am riding with too. I ride with the sway and flow between these three exquisite and ancient beings and I feel and know....

This day provides an opportunity for me to have quick new beginnings and changes and to set intentions in the deepest, darkest, and most pure part of myself. I sink deep to that place that is more pure than pure can be and I find the intention(s) that is coming through for me on this day when the sun and moon and earth pause for a moment in their dance and praise all that is. The intention(s) that comes through is…

On this day in particular, I give much thanks for….

I dance and celebrate….

I feel and acknowledge in this pure vulnerability, the need….

I bow and kiss this pure part of myself and thank it for being so clear, so true in letting me know my most vulnerable truths and for dancing with the songs of all that is...

FRIDAY, JUNE 26, 2020

VENUS STATIONS DIRECT at 6 degrees Gemini

Getting Centered in You

We invite you to start by taking a deep breath, dropping into your true center, your beautiful and pure soul. And from this place, name what is true for you...

Today, I am feeling...

In this moment, what is present for me is...

Today, I am needing...

Today, mine to do is...

Our Message for You

Today, Venus stations direct at 6 degrees of Gemini. Over the past 43 days, since May 13, 2020, Venus has retraced its steps in Gemini, starting at 22 degrees Gemini. Venus is now done with its retrograde period of this year. On this day, we invite you to reflect over the period of the past 43 days and take in anything that has come up for you in your sojourn backward through Gemini. This has been an opportunity for your divine feminine, your sense of values, self value, your sense of beauty, your connection to love to move backward and get a new view of the energies of Gemini - the energies of communication, of learning, of being open to new information, of curiosity, of speaking, writing, and teaching.

The Cosmic Flow Through You

So on this day of Venus stationing direct at 6 degrees in Gemini, I think back over my journey over the past 43 days. I reflect and sink back to May 13, 2020, 43 days ago when Venus went retrograde at 22 degrees of Gemini. I feel into the energies of these past many days. I have reviewed and seen anew...

As Venus stations direct and continues her flow forward in Gemini and then through the remainder of the Zodiac, I feel into her energies as my divine feminine, my sense of beauty, love, money, value, self value and she says to me and through me...

TUESDAY, JUNE 30, 2020

JUPITER AND PLUTO CONJUNCTION
(Second time) at 24 degrees Capricorn

Getting Centered in You

We invite you to start by taking a deep breath, dropping into your true center, your beautiful and pure soul. And from this place, name what is true for you...

Today, I am feeling...

In this moment, what is present for me is...

Today, I am needing...

Today, mine to do is...

Our Message for You

Today, Jupiter and Pluto conjunct for the second time this year at 24 degrees Capricorn. As we mentioned before, on April 4, 2020, this conjunction is very powerful and can feel painful, difficult, can come with a sense or actual events of structures being torn down, both internally and in the world at large. However, this conjunction has a beautiful evolutionary intent. That intent is to give your soul and the collective soul of our world a big push, a big infusion of energy to expand and take a look at the structures of everything that are perhaps collapsing, that need to die, that need to fall away. This second conjunction can be like a wrecking ball hitting the structures that our deepest souls know need to go. It can be like the energies of the cosmos giving us a push to just let it all go, let it all die - whatever needs to die - let it just die. The parts of ourselves that need to go - let them go, let them die. Once again, this could feel painful. It could also feel cathartic or good in some other way. This destruction leaves space in its wake. And we are here to re-build, re-envision our world in exactly whatever ways our deepest souls know we are meant to, right here, right now.

So today is a second wave of the opportunity to feel those structures falling, dying that need to go. And then to try again - see in the empty spaces of those fallen structures what beautiful new vistas or new structures are needed. What are we here to create in place of the old ones? What visions are meant to come through YOU? What are YOU here to create, both within yourself and in the world? "As within, so without," yes? Yes.

So today we invite you to sit with an observing self - what is getting destroyed? What could take shape in its place? What is yours to do in helping to release the old, in helping to envision the new, in helping to build the new moving forward? Sit with these questions and then act accordingly. You are so beautiful. You are meant to be here, right here and right now. We love you and thank you for being you and for doing what you came to this planet to do.

The Cosmic Flow Through You

On this day in which Jupiter conjuncts Pluto for the second time this year, I sit in deep reflection, deep observation. I notice in myself and/or in the world the destruction of many things. On a deeper level, I feel the wisdom of some of this destruction. The things that still need to go, to die are....

Mine to do in this dying process is....

In the wake of the fallen or dying things, I see a vision of what is yet to come. I see....

Mine to do in envisioning this new way is....

Mine to do in creating this new way is....

Today, I....

I bring so many gifts to this world and to this re-creation process. My deepest soul knows that these gifts include....

I bow in deepest gratitude for being given the opportunity to use these gifts in exactly the ways I came to this life to use them and to create in the incredible love I have and feel for this world and for all of creation.

WEDNESDAY, JULY 1, 2020

SATURN RE-ENTERS CAPRICORN going retrograde

Getting Centered in You

We invite you to start by taking a deep breath, dropping into your true center, your beautiful and pure soul. And from this place, name what is true for you...

Today, I am feeling...

In this moment, what is present for me is...

Today, I am needing...

Today, mine to do is...

Our Message for You

Today, Saturn re-enters Capricorn, still going retrograde. As we stated on May 10, 2020, when Saturn went retrograde at 1 degree Aquarius, Saturn dipped its toe into Aquarius as a preview, a taste of what is to come once it moves fully into Aquarius on December 17, 2020, later this year. Now as it heads back into Capricorn for the next five and a half months, we have an opportunity to review and remember the lessons of Saturn in Capricorn that we need and want to take into the "Age of Aquarius" that we are about to truly initiate on December 21 of this year. What are you being asked to sink into, to learn again on a new level, to let go or let take hold in you, to strengthen you as you take part in the re-creation of yourself and of this world?

Saturn in Capricorn is a strong set of energies, because Capricorn is ruled by Saturn, so the energies of Saturn as the elder, wise one, time keeper, task master, and so forth are doubled in a sense. Saturn in Capricorn reminds us of our strength, of our abilities to create solid structure, to keep on task, to do what we set out to do, to face our karma, to get out of our own ways and to "just do it." Saturn in Capricorn can be harsh, can be difficult, but it can also be our friend, can hold our hand to get across the finish line even if we are exhausted. The Saturn and Capricorn energies in us can say, "Hey, you promised to do such and such. You committed to this. You had a vision and you knew and know that your job in all of this is… So get out of bed and do it." And Saturn in Capricorn can help us to understand the "how" and the "when" of all that we envision. Saturn in Aquarius is an amazing visionary and that is where we are headed. However, Saturn in

Capricorn can give us the "umph" and the practical tools to build that vision.

So today, sink into this energy, set the intention to let these energies ride with you. Let yourself ride with your Saturn back into Capricorn, back into whatever energies you are going to need to harness before you and we all head back into Aquarius for the next leg of our amazing, beautiful journey as a collective.

The Cosmic Flow Through You

Today, as Saturn re-enters Capricorn going retrograde, and as Saturn continues to retrograde deeper into Capricorn until it re-enters Aquarius on December 17, 2020, I sink into what deeper lessons I am needing, what guidance I am being asked to accept, both in myself and in the world around me. I notice that as I sink into this energy of Saturn going back into Capricorn, I feel the energies of....

Over the next 5.5 months, I set an intention to be open and receptive to the lessons that Saturn is offering me, giving to me so that I have just the right tools that I need to help build our world in the ways that I am meant to. That intention in the words of my own soul is...

Over these months, I track these lessons, these reflections here. And what I am noticing is....

SATURDAY, JULY 4, 2020

FULL MOON IN CAPRICORN,

13 degrees, 9:44pm, PST
LUNAR ECLIPSE, 13 degrees Capricorn, 9:31pm, PST

Getting Centered in You

We invite you to start by taking a deep breath, dropping into your true center, your beautiful and pure soul. And from this place, name what is true for you...

Today, I am feeling...

In this moment, what is present for me is...

Today, I am needing...

Today, mine to do is...

Our Message for You

Today there is a full moon and lunar eclipse at 13 degrees Capricorn. The energies of this full moon and eclipse again highlight the opportunity to bring through and to harness the lessons of Capricorn and Cancer energies. The sun is in Cancer, shining its light on the fully seen moon in Capricorn. So once again, what are the energies that are needing to be seen, that need to come to full light in these energies balancing the inner, raw and vulnerable wisdom of the light coming from Cancer and the lessons of the Capricorn elder in us all?

Just as you are already listening and observing what Saturn is teaching you as it retrogrades back into Capricorn for the next few months, this full moon in Capricorn also highlights an ability and need to fully see and be seen in the qualities of the strong, firm, and wise energies of Capricorn. What are these energies for you? What are these lessons for you? What are Saturn and the moon and Pluto and Jupiter (currently also conjunct to each other at 23 degrees Capricorn, along with Pallas Athena, also at 23 degrees Capricorn) all giving to you right now? What lessons are there for you, right here, right now. You have many wise elders standing in a line handing you great tools and great gifts. Dive deep and see what it is they are there to show you.

The Cosmic Flow Through You

On this day of a full moon lunar eclipse in Capricorn, when Pallas Athena, Jupiter, Pluto, and Saturn are also in Capricorn, I feel and see a line of wise elders that are aspects of myself and aspects of the cosmic friends we have surrounding us. I close mys eyes and go deep into the place where these wise elders stand and look at me smiling deeply. They hand me gifts, one at a time or all at once. I sit and feel and observe and accept these gifts. The gifts are......

As I sit in the presence of these wise, exquisite elders, I feel......

As I stand in the presence of these wise elder friends, I see and know…..

Mine to do, as a wise elder, myself is….

SUNDAY, JULY 12, 2020

MERCURY GOES DIRECT at 5 degrees Cancer

Getting Centered in You

We invite you to start by taking a deep breath, dropping into your true center, your beautiful and pure soul. And from this place, name what is true for you...

Today, I am feeling...

In this moment, what is present for me is...

Today, I am needing...

Today, mine to do is...

Our Message for You

Today, Mercury finishes its second retrograde period of the year and goes direct at 5 degrees Cancer. It went retrograde on June 18 at 14 degrees Cancer.

As we stated on that day, this retrograde period has been a time for us all to review, revise, reflect, and redo our relationship to the energies of Cancer that are part of us and our world.

Cancer is ruled by the Moon. Similar to the moon, cancer is often sweet and sensitive. Cancer is the sign of the mother and childhood. Cancer is the most vulnerable and inner part of oneself. Cancer is the most raw, truth of who we are deep down, the part of us that needs to be treated tenderly and with honor and great care. Cancer can be watery and emotional, with ups and downs changing in rapid pace. Cancer has great wisdom in what we truly need and can speak purely if we listen with great quiet.

On this day, we invite you to reflect on this time period since June 18, 2020, three and a half weeks ago. What lessons, what insights, what shifts have you felt in yourself or in your world regarding your inner child, your inner most vulnerable and raw self, your home, your sense of home, your mother, your own mothering, the things that nurture you, your nurturing behaviors of yourself and others and of all things?

The Cosmic Flow Through You

On this day in which Mercury goes direct at 5 degrees Cancer, I have had a period of time to internally reflect, revisit, and revise my relationship to the sweet, innocent, pure, vulnerable part of myself, of others, and of our world. As I sit in deep reflection on this today, I notice….

Moving forward, I take with me the lessons of….

I realize that I would like to approach my inner, vulnerable needs differently in these ways....

I feel into these true, inner needs that I have and I honor and hold them. I am rocked and held by existence, by this world. My needs can and are met right here and right now. The sun, the moon, the planets, the stars are all in perfect rhythm and balance all the time and into infinity. And so it is. Thank you.

MONDAY, JULY 20, 2020

NEW MOON IN CANCER, 28 degrees, 10:32am, PST

Getting Centered in You

We invite you to start by taking a deep breath, dropping into your true center, your beautiful and pure soul. And from this place, name what is true for you...

Today, I am feeling...

In this moment, what is present for me is...

Today, I am needing...

Today, mine to do is...

Our Message for You

Once again, the energies of today assist us to reflect, to go deep into our Cancer selves - the parts of us that need nurturing, that need to be held, the parts of us that are nurturing and that do hold others and our world.

As we have stated several times now, Cancer is ruled by the Moon. Similar to the moon, cancer is often sweet and sensitive. Cancer is the sign of the mother and childhood. Cancer is the most vulnerable and inner part of oneself. Cancer is the most raw, truth of who we are deep down, the part of us that needs to be treated tenderly and with honor and great care. Cancer can be watery and emotional, with ups and downs changing in rapid pace. Cancer has great wisdom in what we truly need and can speak purely if we listen with great quiet.

The Cosmic Flow Through You

On this new moon in Cancer, I drop deep into that most precious, vulnerable, held part of myself. I listen for the wisdom of the new intention that I need to set. This is the second new moon in Cancer in a row - the first being at the very beginning of the sign - 0 degrees Cancer, and this one being at the end of the sign at 28 degrees Cancer. Mercury also just completed 3.5 weeks of retrograde in the sign of Cancer, so the cosmic forces have been giving myself and our collective many many chances to reconnect, to revision, to review, and to set intention after intention with regard to our relationship to this beautiful, most vulnerable and purely wise part of ourselves. On this second new moon in Cancer in a row, I feel the call from the deep, quiet part of me that says….

And on this new moon in Cancer, I feels my pure self set the following intention…..

I look back to the last new moon in Cancer just four weeks ago on the summer solstice, June 20, 2020. I remember the energies of that day and my intentions that came forward on that day as well. I notice the shifts in my energy and my relationship to my Cancer energies as they are today. What I observe and feel is....

MONDAY, AUGUST 3, 2020

FULL MOON IN AQUARIUS, 11 degrees, 8:58am, PST

Getting Centered in You

We invite you to start by taking a deep breath, dropping into your true center, your beautiful and pure soul. And from this place, name what is true for you...

Today, I am feeling...

In this moment, what is present for me is...

Today, I am needing...

Today, mine to do is...

Our Message for You

Today is a full moon in Aquarius. Aquarius is ruled by the planet Uranus. Aquarius is innovation. Aquarius is the future. Aquarius moves quickly and is fast and in the realm of the genius and the cosmic. Aquarius comes up with brilliant new ideas and cares a great deal about the collective good. Aquarius is groups and friendships. Aquarius is beautiful and airy and analytical. Aquarius is visionary and can show us things literally of the stars.

The Cosmic Flow Through You

On this day of the full moon in Aquarius, I reflect back to the new moon in Cancer two weeks ago, on July 20, 2020. The intentions I set that day were…

I observe and notice that the energies of the intentions I set on the last new moon have shifted, changed, and/or manifested in….

Today, I also reflect on the energies of Aquarius which are the energies associated with the world we are moving toward creating anew. I feel the sun shining on the full moon and allowing energies of Aquarius in me and in the world to come to full light and full manifestation in whatever way is just right for them today. I feel into the full moon in the sky today and I feel….

I connect to the energies of today's full moon and I feel arise in me….

Aquarius says to me….

A vision I hold today on this full moon is….

TUESDAY, AUGUST 18, 2020

NEW MOON IN LEO, 26 degrees, 7:41pm, PST

Getting Centered in You

We invite you to start by taking a deep breath, dropping into your true center, your beautiful and pure soul. And from this place, name what is true for you...

Today, I am feeling...

In this moment, what is present for me is...

Today, I am needing...

Today, mine to do is...

Our Message for You

Today is a new moon in Leo. Leo is ruled by the Sun. Leo is the king, the queen, the lion, the lioness. Leo is on the stage and loves to be the center of attention. Leo needs to be witnessed and praised. Leo has a big heart and loves to shine and to be seen in that shining way. Leo is creative and relates to all that we create, including our children. Leo can be very loving and also somewhat self centered at times. Leo is expression of all kinds in warm and wonderful ways that need to be seen and need to be shared in our world.

On this day of a new moon in Leo, we offer you the opportunity to sink into your deep, dark, pure self, the place where you can hear your most pure truths. In this place, feel into what is needing and wanting to come forward.

The Cosmic Flow Through You

Today on this new moon in Leo, I am quiet in my deep, pure self and I hear a voice say…

Today on this new moon in Leo, I hear my still, quiet, pure self setting these intentions....

Today I feel into the Leo energies that are me - the part of me that needs and wants to be seen, that needs and wants to shine, like the sun. I feel into my creativity, my expression in the world, my big heart, my ability to love and love and love. I feel myself on the stage, in the limelight, my creative and expressive self shining in exactly the ways I am meant to right here and right now. I fully go into this part of myself and I see, hear, feel, and know....

The Leo new moon says to me...

The Leo new moon nudges me....

The Leo new moon asks me to....

And on this day, I commit to myself, I move with intention to....

And I am loved and seen, fully and completely. I smile big and all of my love that shines into the world comes back and smiles and shines on me too and I feel my own big Leo lion hug.

TUESDAY, SEPTEMBER 1, 2020

FULL MOON IN PISCES, 10 degrees, 10:21pm, PST

Getting Centered in You

We invite you to start by taking a deep breath, dropping into your true center, your beautiful and pure soul. And from this place, name what is true for you...

Today, I am feeling...

In this moment, what is present for me is...

Today, I am needing...

Today, mine to do is...

Our Message for You

Today there is a full moon in Pisces. Pisces is ruled by the planet Neptune and historically by Jupiter. Pisces is the sign of the All that Is. Pisces is ether and the chaos and all knowingness of everything. Pisces is all of existence. Pisces is our intuition, our knowing and divinity and purest love through our hearts. Pisces is the ethereal. Pisces can be related to addiction and depression and despondency. Pisces can help us to channel what needs to come through from all of existence, the spirit world, and the energies of all things. Pisces is beautiful in its own divine way and reminds us that we are all truly one.

Today on this full moon in Pisces, we invite you to shine big, shine beautifully in all of who you are, all of who we all are as one, as all of existence. We also invite you to look back to the intentions you set two weeks ago on the new moon in Leo on August 18, 2020.

The Cosmic Flow Through You

On this day of a full moon in Pisces, I look back to the intentions I set on the new moon in Leo two weeks ago. On that day, the intentions I set were…

Today I look back on those intentions and I see and notice that the energies of those intentions have shifted in these ways…

Today I look to the full moon and I feel beyond the moon into the stars and into the great unknown and the beyond of everything - the chaos, the perfect order of the All That Is and the oneness of everything that is all of us. I feel into these energies of Pisces and what comes through to me is…

The full moon in Pisces wants to manifest and highlight….

The full moon in Pisces wants to remind me and us of….

A vision I have as I feel into the All That Is is....

I remember that I am literally a part of all of existence. The same substances that made the stars made the Earth and made the sun and made the planets and made me. I am a being of the cosmos - literally - as is everyone and everything else. And in this remembrance, I feel and I know, I remember....

My consciousness is huge, is all of everything and I feel the magic, the surprise, the element of beauty in the unknown and in the comfort that everything just is, everything is one, that there is no separation, that I am part of the All That Is and ultimately, all is well. I relax into this ultimate deep peace and let it comfort and soothe me here and now. I am held by existence and all is well.

WEDNESDAY, SEPTEMBER 9, 2020

MARS GOES RETROGRADE, 28 degrees Aries

Getting Centered in You

We invite you to start by taking a deep breath, dropping into your true center, your beautiful and pure soul. And from this place, name what is true for you...

Today, I am feeling...

In this moment, what is present for me is...

Today, I am needing...

Today, mine to do is...

Our Message for You

Today, an unusual phenomenon occurs. Mars has been transiting Aries, a fairly intense, fiery combination considering that Mars rules Aries and that both are energies of fire and the warrior and so forth. Today, Mars retrogrades at 28 degrees Aries and transits backwards in Aries until November 13, 2020 when it will go direct at 15 degrees Aries.

This time period could be intense, potentially difficult, potentially volatile or even violent. However, it also could provide you and us all with an extra boost of energy to initiate, to review, reflect, and to take deep stock of our own relationship to these energies, as well as possibly our individual and collective divine masculine.

In general, Aries is ruled by the planet Mars. Aries is the warrior, the god of war. Aries is fire and "go get 'em" nature. Aries is drive and instinct. Aries charges ahead and penetrates. Aries is a spark that kicks you out of bed and says, "On with it!" Aries gets things started and can catalyze change.

On this day and in the coming two months while Mars is going retrograde in Aries, we invite you to reflect on these energies. What do you notice in yourself regarding energies of initiating, penetrating, jumping out of bed and acting, moving quick and fast, being in touch with your spark of life, your desire to exist, your claiming of your own existence? Take a moment to reflect on your relationship to your own divine masculine. Have you found him? Do you know who he is inside of yourself? If you have found him, when you drop in and feel him, what does he know, what does he say, what does he need, what does his heart feel, his body? What kind of relationship does your divine masculine have to your own divine feminine?

This is a beautiful time to go deep and reflect on these aspects of ourselves and our society, especially as the other energies of this year are encouraging the review and destruction of many power structures that have been based on values of the patriarchy. Our divine masculine is beautiful. He is pure and good. Patriarchy was based on some of the aspects of the divine masculine, but the divine masculine is so much beyond what patriarchy has chosen to be or has come to represent. As Mars goes back through Aries, we encourage you to take this opportunity to mine the gold field of what the deep, real, true divine masculine in yourself and in the collective is really all about. Take this opportunity to love him, to appreciate him, to sit with him, to forgive him, to let his gifts shine, to let him stand firm and tall and strong in this world and in ourselves. Take this opportunity to let the real and true divine masculine to claim his place in this world. Give him the space to come into his own, fully and completely, as the divine, beautiful, loving, strong, gifted, pure being that he is. He is needed. He is wanted. Existence created the divine masculine and the divine feminine as two halves of the same spark, the same spirit, the same full life force. Let this period of time be an opportunity to let the divine masculine to rise in you, in the world. He can and will show up fully. He will stand with the divine feminine and he will show the way with her. They will blend, they will know each other. They will love each other, and they will make a beautiful dance in the sky that they once knew and that they know forever and that will help to heal this world and what it has become. We invite you to allow this dance and this knowing and this mixing to happen in yourself first, then in your most intimate relationships, and then out in the world. This is beautiful and this is why we are here.

The Cosmic Flow Through You

So today, as the beautiful warrior, Mars, goes retrograde in his own sign of Aries, I sink into my own divine masculine. I sink into my own beauty as a fully embodied warrior god who initiates and shows up fully in the world to protect, to give, to stand true and strong, to give power and energy in whatever way it is needed. I love this aspect of myself deeply. I look at him with reverence and love. I forgive the hurts of the masculine and I know that the masculine of Earth is related, but separate from the energy of the divine masculine. As I drop into my Mars energy, he is saying....

As Mars retraces his steps back through his own sign of Aries, I feel and I know and I remember…

Mars, the beautiful, strong warrior carries a gift and remembrance for me. He hands me….

I thank you, beautiful divine masculine. Thank you for showing up. Thank you for being here. Thank you for being present in this world that is healing and that needs you now more than ever. I love you more than I can say.

SATURDAY, SEPTEMBER 12, 2020

JUPITER STATIONS DIRECT, 17 degrees Capricorn

Getting Centered in You

We invite you to start by taking a deep breath, dropping into your true center, your beautiful and pure soul. And from this place, name what is true for you...

Today, I am feeling...

In this moment, what is present for me is...

Today, I am needing...

Today, mine to do is...

Our Message for You

Today, Jupiter goes direct at 17 degrees Capricorn. Since May 14, 2020, Jupiter has been retracing its steps starting at 27 degrees Capricorn. If you remember, on June 30, 2020, Jupiter conjuncted Pluto at 24 degrees of Capricorn as it was in this retrograde sojourn. Now Jupiter has gone back as far as it is going to go before it now heads for its third and final meeting with Pluto which will take place on November 12, 2020, and then for its entrance into Aquarius on December 17, 2020 and its conjunction with Saturn at 0 degrees Aquarius on December 21, 2020.

As Jupiter moves forward back through Capricorn and toward its third and final meeting with Pluto in this year and in this Jupiter cycle, and as Jupiter also picks up steam to head for its committed journey into Aquarius, we invite you to pick up your last needed tools of the trade and lessons of this time of Jupiter in Capricorn. What lessons, reminders, or tools are the energies of Capricorn still needing to give you at this time? What lessons or reminders about your wise elder self, your ability to work hard, to commit to completing what you set out to do, and so forth are waiting for you?

Feel into this and observe what you feel, hear, see, and know in this time.

The Cosmic Flow Through You

On this day as Jupiter stations direct at 17 degrees Capricorn and heads toward its third and final meeting with Pluto at 22 degrees Capricorn and then its entry into Aquarius, I review the experiences, feelings, and lessons of this year so far. I look back to April 4, 2020, when Jupiter first met up with Pluto at 24 degrees of Capricorn. I then look back to June 30, 2020 when Jupiter retraced its steps through Capricorn and then met up with Pluto again. Jupiter has continued its move backward through Capricorn, has picked up strength and information in this sign of Capricorn and is now ready to do what it needs to do in concert with the transformation of this planet. This may be in massive ways. It might be on subtle levels. I feel into my experience of these energies and this travelling trajectory of Jupiter over the past many months and I observe, I feel, I notice....

As Jupiter turns direct and picks up steam, I feel him heading back toward his friend and co-worker, the deeply transformative planet of Pluto. In this moment, Jupiter says....

I take a deep breath and hear the dance of the cosmos. I feel and know what is mine to do in this dance right here and right now. Mine to do is....

I give thanks for the transformations that are taking place, that need to take place, and for the ultimate potential for rebuilding of this world and of ourselves in ways that we have needed for a long, long time. I take a breath and come back to my part in the transformation and the rebuilding. I am surrounded by all that I need to have strength and focus and drive and commitment to this change, to why I came to this planet, and for why I am here right here and right now. I move forward with an open heart, a committed and consistent drive to be present and active in exactly what is mine to do. And so it is.

THURSDAY, SEPTEMBER 17, 2020

NEW MOON IN VIRGO, 25 degrees, 4:00am, PST

Getting Centered in You

We invite you to start by taking a deep breath, dropping into your true center, your beautiful and pure soul. And from this place, name what is true for you...

Today, I am feeling...

In this moment, what is present for me is...

Today, I am needing...

Today, mine to do is...

Our Message for You

Today is the new moon in Virgo. Virgo is ruled by Mercury, just like Gemini. Virgo is beautiful. Virgo is discriminating. Virgo can be a true healer. Virgo is down to earth and practical. Virgo is diligent and works hard. Virgo is persistent and methodical. Virgo is self contained and perceptive. Virgo is clean and clears out what is no longer needed. Virgo is reliable and true.

On this new moon in Virgo, we feel an opportunity for you to take a break perhaps from the intense, somewhat relentless energies lately of Pluto and Jupiter in Capricorn, Mars going retrograde in Aries, and so forth, and to relax and rejuvenate for a minute in the clean, healing, responsibilities energies of Virgo. Relax into this part of you. You can count on the part of you that is a healthy Virgo. Virgo takes care of your body, is clean and clear, and can help you to discriminate in all kinds of ways, including that which is best to carry forward and that which you can and maybe should leave behind.

Today we invite you especially to take stock of this year so far which may have been rather intense for you and perhaps for the world. Let the energies of Virgo clean you, cleanse you, give you a bath, give you a nice healing treatment, look at you as the pure, clean soul that you are in the stars and also here on Earth.

The Cosmic Flow Through You

On this day of the new moon in Virgo, I close my eyes, take a deep breath, and sink into the energies of Virgo in me. I might be tired. I might have been working hard on a human and soul level. And I let go. I let Virgo clean and clear away anything and everything that I no longer need to carry with me on this journey moving forward. I trust her to discern what I need and what I don't. Virgo just rocks me, cleans me, wipes my brow, heals me. And I rest for as long as I need in this quiet still point of this new moon. I go deep, deep deep into myself in the deep, most clean and pure part of myself and I notice leaving me....

In this place, I notice what Virgo is clearing. I notice that in her wisdom, I see...

I give gratitude for the ability to rest and come to this place in myself of discernment, of healing, of cleaning and clearing myself and my life.

MONDAY, SEPTEMBER 28, 2020

SATURN STATIONS DIRECT at 25 degrees Capricorn

Getting Centered in You

We invite you to start by taking a deep breath, dropping into your true center, your beautiful and pure soul. And from this place, name what is true for you...

Today, I am feeling...

In this moment, what is present for me is...

Today, I am needing...

Today, mine to do is...

Our Message for You

Today, Saturn stations direct at 25 degrees Capricorn. Pluto is going retrograde at 22 degrees Capricorn, Jupiter is going direct at 17 degrees Capricorn, Mars is precisely squaring Saturn and going retrograde at 25 degrees of Aries, nearly conjunct Eris who is also going retrograde at 24 degrees Aries. In addition, Venus is precisely trining Mars at 25 degrees Leo. This is an intense and firey combination that means business. However, Mars and Venus trining each other in this way also adds an element of beautiful harmony and a commitment to manifest this creative and harmonious potential in the world.

Overall, today we invite you to sink into all of these energies and notice what you are being called to move forward to do. This is a great number of energies, seeming to work in opposing forces in some ways, but actually all working in concert toward one goal - the goal of evolution that we all came to work toward. Think of all of these energies as pulleys on a complex machine. They might seem to be pulling in all different directions, but they are actually beautifully complex and are part of a design that we can barely comprehend, if at all.

Simply take a moment to take a deep breath and drop into what is yours to do today. As Saturn stations direct, he is heading back toward Aquarius which he will enter finally in two and a half months on December 17, 2020. He is doing a dance with Pluto, Jupiter, Mars, Venus, and all of the other planets and of course with all of existence, just as we all are. Saturn is giving us a chance to pick up any and all lessons we will need as he finally enters Aquarius in just over two months. What are these lessons for you? What do you have left to pick up and see fresh or again regarding the energies related to conscious work, conscious drive to get things done, complete what you set out to do, to do things at just the right timing, to take time to do things thoroughly and well, and so forth? Take a minute to drop in and feel into this for yourself.

The Cosmic Flow Through You

Today, as Saturn stations direct at 25 degrees Capricorn and plays its complex dance in the cosmos, I drop into its song, its dance and I feel, I remember, Saturn says….

I carry with me the intentions I have set over this whole past year and of my whole existence, for that matter, and I pick up the tools I need to carry forward and to do what I came to do. Those tools include....

I think back to the visions I have had this year of the new world we are committed to sharing and to re-building and I remember that my commitment and mine to do in this rebuilding is....

I give thanks that I am given the exact tools I need at this exact moment I need them and that the dance of the cosmos is constantly in a perfect dance with me to help me do exactly what is mine to do, here and now and in every moment.

THURSDAY, OCTOBER 1, 2020

FULL MOON IN ARIES, 9 degrees, 2:05pm, PST

Getting Centered in You

We invite you to start by taking a deep breath, dropping into your true center, your beautiful and pure soul. And from this place, name what is true for you...

Today, I am feeling...

In this moment, what is present for me is...

Today, I am needing...

Today, mine to do is...

Our Message for You

Today is a full moon in Aries. Aries is ruled by the planet Mars. Aries is the warrior, the god of war. Aries is fire and "go get 'em" nature. Aries is drive and instinct. Aries charges ahead and penetrates. Aries is a spark that kicks you out of bed and says, "On with it!" Aries gets things started and can catalyze change.

Today I feel into the energies of the sun shining its light on the moon in Aries. The moon feels and knows this part of me - the part that is fiery and that same divine masculine that I am feeling into as Mars is still going retrograde through Aries as well.

The Cosmic Flow Through You

Today I feel into my goddess friend of the moon and listen to what she is needing me to show to the world in my Aries, divine masculine self. The moon shows…

Today I think back to the intentions I set on the last new moon which was on September 17, 2020 and was in the sign of Virgo. The intentions I set on that day were…

I feel into and remember those intentions I set on that last new moon and I notice that those energies and intentions have shifted and changed over the past two weeks in these ways….

SUNDAY, OCTOBER 4, 2020

PLUTO STATIONS DIRECT at 22 degrees Capricorn

Getting Centered in You

We invite you to start by taking a deep breath, dropping into your true center, your beautiful and pure soul. And from this place, name what is true for you...

Today, I am feeling...

In this moment, what is present for me is...

Today, I am needing...

Today, mine to do is...

Our Message for You

Today, Pluto stations direct at 22 degrees Capricorn. Pluto has been going retrograde since April 25, 2020 when it turned direct at 24 degrees Capricorn. During this time, Jupiter conjunct Pluto for a second time on June 30, 2020 at 24 degrees Capricorn.

The Cosmic Flow Through You

Over the past 5.5 months, my soul has had a chance to revisit and review its deepest values and to let go and transform in some massive ways. These areas of transformation have been…

I take with myself the lessons of…

I feel the deep knowledge of my soul. My soul says....

And I feel the deep soul of our planet and of existence and it says....

TUESDAY, OCTOBER 13, 2020

MERCURY GOES RETROGRADE at
11 degrees Scorpio

Getting Centered in You

We invite you to start by taking a deep breath, dropping into your true center, your beautiful and pure soul. And from this place, name what is true for you...

Today, I am feeling...

In this moment, what is present for me is...

Today, I am needing...

Today, mine to do is...

Our Message for You

Today Mercury goes retrograde at 11 degrees Scorpio. This is the third mercury retrograde of this year. As we have stated on the previous days of mercury going retrograde, mercury retrograde can be a funny time. It often has the reputation of causing many "issues" and problems with communication and technology. This certainly can be true. One association with the energy of something going "retrograde" can be that it is going "backward" or doing the wrong thing. However, the energy of something "retrograding" is also that it is going "backward" in the sense that it is backing up and giving us a chance to reflect, to review, to do something again in a new and different, more evolved way.

This time, Mercury is going retrograde in the sign of Scorpio and will go direct at 25 degrees of Libra on November 3, 2020, in just over three weeks. So the flavor of this mercury is very different and distinct from the previous two. The first mercury retrograde retraced through the sign of Pisces and into Aquarius. The second one sojourned backward through the sign of Cancer. And this time mercury is retracing his steps back through Scorpio and is dipping into the end degrees of Libra. This particular journey of mercury gives us all a chance to review and reflect on our relationship to the energies of Scorpio and then Libra. The review of the energies of Scorpio pairs well with the recent retrograde of Pluto as Pluto rules Scorpio and their energies are similar.

Scorpio is ruled by the planet Pluto and historically ruled by Mars. Scorpio is deep and dark. Scorpio is related to the underworld, the areas of depth and death that people often are afraid of. Scorpio is incredibly perceptive and likes to bring up and talk about things that often get left unsaid or unnamed. Scorpio is the taboo. Scorpio is death. Scorpio is the deep healer, the medicine man and medicine woman, the sage, the elder of the deep, the shaman. Scorpio has a deep magic and incredible power. Scorpio helps things to die over and over and over again and is crucial in assisting us to let go of anything that is no longer serving the deepest, most true evolution of our soul.

Libra is ruled by Venus, just as Taurus is. Libra is a kind of beauty, slightly different in quality from earthy, beautiful Virgo. Libra is balanced and in tune with the other. Libra is the sign related to partnerships of all kinds, of working and balancing with the others, including in marriage partnerships. Libra likes harmony and can be co-dependent. Libra often needs to balance with its polarity of Aries to learn to be independent while also interdependent. Libra is a wonderful listener and can truly understand all sides of a situation. Libra is a great mediator and friend.

So today and during this 3.5 week period of mercury returning through these two signs, we invite you to sink into and notice what comes up for you, especially in relation to your communication and learning with regard to your Scorpio and Libra energies. What do you feel and notice during this time?

The Cosmic Flow Through You

Today and over the next 3.5 weeks while mercury is travelling retrograde through Scorpio and Libra, I sink into and ride along with Mercury and notice what he is showing me, teaching me how my communications of all kinds might be asked to review or do things in a new way, especially with regard to my deep soul and my sense of beauty and both harmony and merging with others, as well as the other energies of Scorpio and Libra.

What I see and notice today and during this period is…

FRIDAY, OCTOBER 16, 2020

NEW MOON IN LIBRA, 23 degrees, 12:30pm, PST

Getting Centered in You

We invite you to start by taking a deep breath, dropping into your true center, your beautiful and pure soul. And from this place, name what is true for you...

Today, I am feeling...

In this moment, what is present for me is...

Today, I am needing...

Today, mine to do is...

Our Message for You

Today there is a new moon in Libra at 23 degrees. This pairs interestingly with mercury who is going retrograde backward through Scorpio and then heading into Libra during this period as well. As we have said earlier, Libra is ruled by Venus, just as Taurus is. Libra is a kind of beauty, slightly different in quality from earthy, beautiful Virgo. Libra is balanced and in tune with the other. Libra is the sign related to partnerships of all kinds, of working and balancing with the others, including in marriage partnerships. Libra likes harmony and can be co-dependent. Libra often needs to balance with its polarity of Aries to learn to be independent while also interdependent. Libra is a wonderful listener and can truly understand all sides of a situation. Libra is a great mediator and friend.

The Cosmic Flow Through You

On this day of a new moon in Libra, I sink into the deep, dark quiet place inside myself. I feel a click with that most pure part of me and I hear the still, soft voice that is my truest self say....

I feel into this dark, quiet place in me and I feel myself setting the intentions of....

I feel into the energies of Libra and Libra says through me....

I feel into the parts of me that are Libra like energies and I embrace them and embody them. I feel them help my body and help me to know....

I feel gratitude and harmony within myself and I feel a balance between my need for independence and my need and desire for interdependence. I find this balance in my body, in my heart, in my soul, and in my relationships in the world. This balance is beautiful and feels like....

I give gratitude for the ability and the option to always come back to this balance that is ultimately a mirror of the balance and dance of all things in existence. Thank you and thank you and thank you. And so it is....

SATURDAY, OCTOBER 31, 2020

FULL MOON IN TAURUS, 8 degrees, 7:49pm, PST

Getting Centered in You

We invite you to start by taking a deep breath, dropping into your true center, your beautiful and pure soul. And from this place, name what is true for you...

Today, I am feeling...

In this moment, what is present for me is...

Today, I am needing...

Today, mine to do is...

Our Message for You

Today is a full moon in Taurus. Taurus is ruled by the planet Venus. Taurus is "the bull." Taurus is the grounded, sensual nature of home and clothing and textures. Taurus likes being fixed and earthy. Taurus loves to curl up with a book and stay cozy in a warm bed. Taurus is sensual and sexual in the physical world. Taurus loves beautiful things and loves to be held and touched. Taurus loves a good massage and the smell of gorgeous flowers and the sun on the skin. Taurus is steady and true.

We just had a new moon in Libra which is also a sign ruled by Venus. So this whole cycle of the moon, starting with that new moon in Libra two weeks gives us an interesting opportunity to be in a closer relationship to our Venus, our divine feminine. Mars is still going retrograde through Aries, highlighting our relationship to our own divine masculine. This lunar cycle gives an interesting opportunity to also focus on our relationship to the divine feminine. What does she feel and look like inside you and in relation to you?

Take time to reflect in this way, to feel into and embody your own exquisite beauty - just perfect, just exactly as you are. What does this full moon in Taurus call out in you to shine to the world regarding your self value, your beauty, your gorgeous and perfect body, your sensuality, your sexuality, your desire to be touched and to have pleasurable feelings and sensations in your world and in your home and in your life? These are all legitimate and important needs and they hold wisdom. Allow them to talk to and through you today and during this lunar cycle and always for that matter. This is a crucial part of who you are.

The Cosmic Flow Through You

On this full moon in Taurus, I sink into my body and give thanks for how perfect and beautiful it is, just the way it is. It is carrying an expression of my soul and I love and hold my body in its perfection and I listen to what it needs and wants and what wisdom it holds, right here and right now. As I sink into myself on this full moon in Taurus, I feel and hear myself saying....

I tune into the big, beautiful full moon in Taurus and she is curvy and sensual and she speaks through me, saying...

I open and accept reminders of my beauty and of my self worth and of the love surrounding me at all times. I allow in reminders of this at all times. As I feel into all that surrounds, loves, supports, and reminds me of my perfection and my beauty, I feel and hear and see....

I am perfect. I am whole. I am home. I am beautiful just exactly as who and how I am, right here, right now. The cosmos created me, just as perfectly as it created every star, just as it created every planet and the moon, and this Earth herself. I am whole and carry with me this perfection of the All That Is at all times. And so it is. Thank you...

TUESDAY, NOVEMBER 3, 2020

MERCURY GOES DIRECT at 25 degrees Libra

Getting Centered in You

We invite you to start by taking a deep breath, dropping into your true center, your beautiful and pure soul. And from this place, name what is true for you...

Today, I am feeling...

In this moment, what is present for me is...

Today, I am needing...

Today, mine to do is...

Our Message for You

Today, Mercury goes direct at 25 degrees Libra. Over the past 3.5 weeks, Mercury has reviewed and retraced its steps through the first half of Scorpio and the end degrees of Libra. Over this time period, what has come up for you with regard to your relationship to the energies of Scorpio and Libra?

As we stated on October 13, 2020 when Mercury first went retrograde in this cycle, Scorpio is ruled by the planet Pluto and historically ruled by Mars. Scorpio is deep and dark. Scorpio is related to the underworld, the areas of depth and death that people often are afraid of. Scorpio is incredibly perceptive and likes to bring up and talk about things that often get left unsaid or unnamed. Scorpio is the taboo. Scorpio is death. Scorpio is the deep healer, the medicine man and medicine woman, the sage, the elder of the deep, the shaman. Scorpio has a deep magic and incredible power. Scorpio helps things to die over and over and over again and is crucial in assisting us to let go of anything that is no longer serving the deepest, most true evolution of our soul.

Libra is ruled by Venus, just as Taurus is. Libra is a kind of beauty, slightly different in quality from earthy, beautiful Virgo. Libra is balanced and in tune with the other. Libra is the sign related to partnerships of all kinds, of working and balancing with the others, including in marriage partnerships. Libra likes harmony and can be co-dependent. Libra often needs to balance with its polarity of Aries to learn to be independent while also interdependent. Libra is a wonderful listener and can truly understand all sides of a situation. Libra is a great mediator and friend.

The Cosmic Flow Through You

I think back to October 13, 2020 and the 3.5 weeks since then. I sink into what knowledge I have gained, what lessons I have reviewed or learned, what parts of myself have changed and transformed and what I notice is….

THURSDAY, NOVEMBER 12, 2020

JUPITER AND PLUTO CONJUNCTION
(for the THIRD time this year) at 22 degrees Capricorn

Getting Centered in You

We invite you to start by taking a deep breath, dropping into your true center, your beautiful and pure soul. And from this place, name what is true for you...

Today, I am feeling...

In this moment, what is present for me is...

Today, I am needing...

Today, mine to do is...

Our Message for You

Today is November 12, 2020, the third and final conjunction of Jupiter and Pluto in Capricorn in this year and in this cycle between Jupiter and Pluto. This third conjunction is at 22 degrees of Capricorn, rather than at 24 degrees of Capricorn of the previous two as Pluto went retrograde over much of this year and is now still back at 22 degrees of Capricorn.

In this third and final conjunction of Jupiter and Pluto in Capricorn, it is as though this is Jupiter's third and final pass, final blow, or final meeting with the deep soul of ourselves and of our collective and of existence. It is as though Jupiter is either consulting as a friend or is giving a blow as a force of evolution and of growth to give a final push to whatever needs to go, whatever needs to be expanded and cleared out to make room for the new structures that we are all being given the opportunity to create.

Once again, as in the previous two conjunctions between Pluto and Jupiter, this conjunction could feel like a blow, could be experienced as traumatic, or could be experienced as a supportive, expansive hand holding us up, helping us to really do this - to really let go and let go and let go of whatever needs to die, needs to release in us and in our world. This is especially true with regard to any and all structures both in ourselves and in our societies and in our world.

So in this time that could be feeling particular intense or difficult or trying or painful (or not!), we invite you to remember the big picture. We invite you to let go of any desire to control the outcome of this particular time. This is still a time of dying, of letting go, so that very soon the new can come in. And it will.

You have set the tone, you have set the stage, you have envisioned and practiced this whole year. You have done deep work. You have done amazing work. You are ready. Just let these last pieces die that need to die. Let it all go. You are ok. All is ok. You are here to help to be part of this letting go and dying process. That is why you are here, right here and right now. And you are here to be part of the birthing process as well. Pluto is about death and birth, both in the deepest, often most painful parts of you and of existence. Remember that birth and death are both part of the same thing. Let everything die and soon will be time for a birth that you came to witness and to midwife as well. Just let the dying process complete, finish, come to a complete end of its cycle. Be gentle with yourself and with this. It is all ok. It is part of life. It is part of what needs to happen right here and right now. And we are so grateful to you for being here. We are here with you as well.

The Cosmic Flow Through You

On this day as Jupiter conjuncts Pluto for the third and final time in Capricorn, I feel into what I am still allowing to die, what is still needing to die in me and in my world. I feel....

This dying and letting go feels like....

As the old dies away and makes room for the birth of what is coming next, I am surrounded by midwives of existence. They are here also to assist with this death and birth process, both, as they are one and the same. I am surrounded by....

I am held and supported, right here and right now. And when it is time to be present for the birthing process, I will be ready and held and supported then too.

FRIDAY, NOVEMBER 13, 2020

MARS STATIONS DIRECT at 15 degrees Aries

Getting Centered in You

We invite you to start by taking a deep breath, dropping into your true center, your beautiful and pure soul. And from this place, name what is true for you...

Today, I am feeling...

In this moment, what is present for me is...

Today, I am needing...

Today, mine to do is...

Our Message for You

Today, Mars goes direct at 15 degrees Aries. Over the past months as Mars has been going retrograde in Aries, it is as though the divine masculine has been given a chance to rejuvenate, to refortify itself, just in time for the final dying process that is occurring right now as Jupiter made its final conjunction with Pluto yesterday and is now heading for its move into Aquarius that will happen in just over a month.

It is as though Mars and the divine masculine have had a chance to recharge and refortify himself to now be present for the collective move into the coming weeks when we will complete the last laps of this year and this deep time of transformation, of death, of beauty, and of re-visioning and of trying on what we came to create. Now as Mars goes direct, he is able to bring all of his passion, all of his fire, all of his energy to initiate, to give direction, to penetrate, to move forward with precision and care, to go full steam ahead toward and then into this new age we are all collectively creating.

The Cosmic Flow Through You

On this day and moving forward, as Mars goes direct at 15 degrees of Aries, I feel into this fire inside of me. I feel into my divine masculine who I love and into the pure, divine masculine of the collective and of existence. I look into his eyes and I feel his beauty and his strength. I feel his commitment to this world and I feel all of the healing he has been and is continuing to do. I feel him showing up in the world and in turning his attention to this task ahead - that of creating the world we all came to create.

I feel into the divine masculine that is in me and he is saying....

I feel into the divine masculine of the collective and he is saying, doing, and showing...

I am held in myself and with the collective by this divine masculine. I feel the balance of the divine masculine and the divine feminine righting itself. I feel the harmony of those two healing at lightening speed and coming into a beautiful, ultimate and divine working relationship with each other that is needed on this planet right here and right now. I feel this inside myself and in the world at large. It is beautiful and I am so grateful. I breathe in the balance. I breathe in the healing. I breathe in the divine love. I breathe in the divine beauty of it all. And so it is.

SATURDAY, NOVEMBER 14, 2020

NEW MOON IN SCORPIO, 23 degrees, 9:07pm, PST

Getting Centered in You

We invite you to start by taking a deep breath, dropping into your true center, your beautiful and pure soul. And from this place, name what is true for you...

Today, I am feeling...

In this moment, what is present for me is...

Today, I am needing...

Today, mine to do is...

Our Message for You

Today is a new moon in Scorpio. As we have said earlier, Scorpio is ruled by the planet Pluto and historically ruled by Mars. Scorpio is deep and dark. Scorpio is related to the underworld, the areas of depth and death that people often are afraid of. Scorpio is incredibly perceptive and likes to bring up and talk about things that often get left unsaid or unnamed. Scorpio is the taboo. Scorpio is death. Scorpio is the deep healer, the medicine man and medicine woman, the sage, the elder of the deep, the shaman. Scorpio has a deep magic and incredible power. Scorpio helps things to die over and over and over again and is crucial in assisting us to let go of anything that is no longer serving the deepest, most true evolution of our soul.

The Cosmic Flow Through You

On this day of a new moon in Scorpio, I drop into my deepest, dark, wise and knowing part of my soul. My soul is in concert with the energies of Scorpio. I hear what intentions need to come through me today. Those intentions are…

The new moon says through me….

The energies of Scorpio say through me….

Scorpio brings through again the opportunity for things to die that need to go. I take a deep breath and feel the following ready to transform and go….

I trust my soul, I trust my deepest wisdom and the deepest wisdom of existence. I give thanks for evolution and for the opportunity to change and grow just as I came to this life to do. And so it is. Thank you.

MONDAY, NOVEMBER 30, 2020

FULL MOON IN GEMINI, 8 degrees, 1:29am, PST
LUNAR ECLIPSE, 8 degrees Gemini, 1:44pm, PST

Getting Centered in You

We invite you to start by taking a deep breath, dropping into your true center, your beautiful and pure soul. And from this place, name what is true for you...

Today, I am feeling...

In this moment, what is present for me is...

Today, I am needing...

Today, mine to do is...

Our Message for You

Today is a full moon and lunar eclipse in Gemini. Gemini is ruled by the planet Mercury. Gemini is a communicator. Gemini loves to talk and think and speak and write and say whatever is on its mind. Gemini loves to learn and has to do with childhood, siblings, and primary school. Gemini can think fast, is an air sign, and can be flighty, moving from thing to thing to thing to thing. Gemini is often curious and inquisitive. Gemini can be dualistic and secretive. Gemini can also be a great explainer of details and important information. Gemini is a great energy for helping the world to understand many things better.

This eclipse in Gemini harkens back to earlier this year when there was a first eclipse in Gemini on June 5, 2020. Then on June 20, 2020, there was an eclipse at 0 degrees Cancer, but the nodes of the moon were at 29 degrees of Gemini and Sagittarius. Look back to those eclipse times, both of them, although in particular the one on June 5, 2020. Feel into that whole time period - one month beforehand and six months since (so up through now). Look back at what energies and messages were coming through for you then and how those energies have changed and shifted since then. What do you notice? How have you changed and grown? How have your life circumstances changed or evolved in that time?

The Cosmic Flow Through You

On this day when there is a full moon and lunar eclipse at 8 degrees Gemini, I feel back over the past months since the eclipse in Gemini on June 5, 2020. I remind myself of the energies and intentions I set on that day and over that time period. Those energies and intentions were....

Today on this full moon lunar eclipse, I am being called to bring through possibly radical change. The energies I feel moving through me and my life and the world today are....

Today, I also think back two weeks to the new moon in Scorpio. The intentions I set then were...

I feel into those energies and intentions and I notice and feel....

I move into the last month of this year and get ready for major movement and change as we all traverse this coming month. The energies, truth, and wisdom coming through me today are....

I am ready. Let's do it.

MONDAY, DECEMBER 14, 2020

NEW MOON IN SAGITTARIUS,
23 degrees, 8:16am, PST

TOTAL SOLAR ECLIPSE in
Sagittarius, 23 degrees, 8:14am, PST
(Sun, Moon, Mercury conjunct South Node in Sagittarius)

Getting Centered in You

We invite you to start by taking a deep breath, dropping into your true center, your beautiful and pure soul. And from this place, name what is true for you...

Today, I am feeling...

In this moment, what is present for me is...

Today, I am needing...

Today, mine to do is...

Our Message for You

Today is a new moon and total solar eclipse in Sagittarius. Today, the sun, moon, mercury are all near the south node in Sagittarius. This brings through a powerful set of energies as Mercury joins the party of the eclipse, opposite the sign of Gemini which is ruled by Mercury. This eclipse has the potential to bring through great energies and change regarding the energies of Sagittarius, but also of Gemini, with the energies conjunct the south node being directed to the north node in Gemini.

Sagittarius is ruled by Jupiter. Sagittarius is big and boisterous and expansive. Sagittarius is the leader, teacher, guru. Sagittarius is the big, wide world, the explorer energy, the part of us that wants to go and try out new foods, new ways, immerse in new languages and places and perhaps become something that we never thought we could be before. Sagittarius is the "foreign." Sagittarius is luck and exaggeration at the same time. Sagittarius has to do with beliefs and religion and sometimes dogma. Sagittarius has to do with truth and can sometimes stretch the truth. Sagittarius can help us to discern our own truth and to speak it to the world.

As we have reviewed many times this year, Gemini is ruled by the planet Mercury. Gemini is a communicator. Gemini loves to talk and think and speak and write and say whatever is on its mind. Gemini loves to learn and has to do with childhood, siblings, and primary school. Gemini can think fast, is an air sign, and can be flighty, moving from thing to thing to thing to thing. Gemini is often curious and inquisitive. Gemini can be dualistic and secretive. Gemini can also be a great explainer of details and important information. Gemini is a great energy for helping the world to understand many things better.

Today, we invite you to feel into your energies of Sagittarius, especially in conjunction with the energies of Mercury, the communicator and learner.

✵

The Cosmic Flow Through You

Today I feel the sun in a full eclipse and the powerful energies this harnesses and brings through. The energies I feel moving through me today are....

The energies I feel moving through the world today are....

When I feel into the energies of Sagittarius and my ability to communicate and to be in learning mode, especially with regard to the energies of Sagittarius, I feel...

As we come close to the final, powerful energies of 2020, this eclipse is bringing through the needed energies and lessons of.....

THURSDAY, DECEMBER 17, 2020

SATURN RE-ENTERS AQUARIUS (for the second time in 2020)

Getting Centered in You

We invite you to start by taking a deep breath, dropping into your true center, your beautiful and pure soul. And from this place, name what is true for you...

Today, I am feeling...

In this moment, what is present for me is...

Today, I am needing...

Today, mine to do is...

Our Message for You

Today is the beginning of a party. Today Saturn re-enters Aquarius, this time not just for a quick dip as it did earlier this year, but for a committed journey into the full sign of Aquarius. It will soon conjunct Jupiter in just four days, a conjunction that many feel is the spark and real beginning of the Age of Aquarius.

This is an exciting time that holds a great deal of potential. As we have reviewed many times this year, the energy of Saturn entering Aquarius is that of a wise visionary. The collective cosmic energies are calling you and all of us to fully embody this part of yourself. You have shed, destroyed, let go, and let die so many old ways in yourself over this past year and over your life for that matter. Today is the beginning of stepping fully into the part of you that came here to bring wisdom and vision onto this planet in the way that only you can.

So today simply feel into that self that is your wise elder visionary. Feel into who she or he is. Describe her or him in detail. Feel her or him fully. Completely embody every aspect of him/her.

The Cosmic Flow Through You

Today as Saturn re-enters Aquarius and heads toward its celebratory conjunction with Jupiter in just four days, I feel deeply into my wise, elder visionary self. I feel every aspect of this part of myself. I see through her eyes. I hear through his ears. I know what she knows. I embody every single aspect of him. What I feel, see, hear, and embody is….

The wise elder visionary that I am is….

The wise elder visionary who I am knows….

SATURDAY, DECEMBER 19, 2020

JUPITER ENTERS AQUARIUS

Getting Centered in You

We invite you to start by taking a deep breath, dropping into your true center, your beautiful and pure soul. And from this place, name what is true for you...

Today, I am feeling...

In this moment, what is present for me is...

Today, I am needing...

Today, mine to do is...

Our Message for You

Today Jupiter enters Aquarius! Similar to two days ago when Saturn entered Aquarius, this is now part two of building up to a party! This is the first time that Jupiter has been in Aquarius in almost twelve years. The last time Jupiter entered Aquarius was on January 5, 2009.

Today as Jupiter enters Aquarius, he adds his majesty and his grandeur and his vision and his ability to magnify things to the energies of Aquarius.

Jupiter is heading toward a conjunction and new phase with Saturn in just two days at 0 degrees Aquarius. We will discuss that further on that day.

However, on today, we invite you simply to feel into and anchor into yourself the part of you that is the grand guru, the teacher, the leader, the explorer, the scholar visionary that is Jupiter in Aquarius. This part of you is necessary, is key to bringing through all of the wisdom and knowledge you have gained in your intense and possibly at times painful journey over the past year. This is a day to simply sink into a very positive energy that is within you - the part of you that can see into the future - the part of you that explores the world and all of the cosmos and that knows how to be far reaching and present at the same time - the part of you that knows how to teach these great learnings and how to spread this knowledge far and wide. Sink into and appreciate this part of yourself and simply give this part of you a deep, big, wide smile and say, "Thank you and welcome."

The Cosmic Flow Through You

On this day, I welcome home the part of myself that is the grand guru, teacher, leader, explorer, scholar visionary of Jupiter in Aquarius. I sink into this part of myself and I feel…

I sink into this energy that is part of who I am and I fully embody it as well. This part of me sees far. I see….

As this part of me comes through for the ride into the creation of this new world, this part of me knows and brings….

I give great gratitude for this and all parts of myself as I harness all of my lessons, all of the knowledge I have gleaned over this past year. I am ready. I am present. I am exactly who and what and where I am meant to be right here and right now. And so it is.

MONDAY, DECEMBER 21, 2020

WINTER/SUMMER SOLSTICE
JUPITER AND SATURN CONJUNCT at
0 degrees, 29 minutes Aquarius

Getting Centered in You

We invite you to start by taking a deep breath, dropping into your true center, your beautiful and pure soul. And from this place, name what is true for you...

Today, I am feeling...

In this moment, what is present for me is...

Today, I am needing...

Today, mine to do is...

Our Message for You

Today is the day! Happy Solstice!!!

This is the day that we have been looking forward to all year!

On this day, Jupiter conjuncts Saturn at 0 degrees and 29 minutes of Aquarius. Many believe this to be the sign of the beginning of the Aquarian Age - a 2000 year age in the cycle of great ages of life on this planet. Your planet has been transitioning out of what many of you have called the Age of Pisces. As we explained in our introduction to this journal, the energies of the Age of Aquarius are varied and can take shape in many different ways depending on your free will individually, as societies, and as a collective, as well as the collective efforts of all of us in all of existence. Remember that what is happening on your planet is simply part of a shift of energies in all of existence. Remember that this time is akin to the energies in your part of existence shifting from being on the "down end" of a teeter totter. The energies in your part of existence has been relatively dense, packed together, have felt heavy and more focused on "three dimensional reality" which you know is only one tiny part of the ultimate reality of infinite dimensional reality.

What you are calling The Age of Aquarius is essentially the shifting of these energies in your part of existence to lighten up the teeter totter, balance it more toward center and allow the densities of your part of existence to open up, to lighten up, to have more space and more room and to allow in the infinite realities to come back into play in your world and in your part of existence.

So this is what is happening today and in this whole time period. It started many years ago and this shift is actually gradual, but today marks a spark, a clicking of energies that signifies a new beginning, a new way of relating in the world, in your solar system, in your galaxy.

Today marks a shift and a movement into a way of being that allows a lightening of possibilities. Today marks a new way of being that will bring into being many many more of the infinite dimensions, the infinite possibilities, the infinite layers of reality and of existence in all times and all places.

The balance and opening up of these energies is not instantaneous and is not fated to manifest in any particular way. It will still take work. That is why you are here. You are here to be the foot soldiers, the way showers, the pavers of the new way. You are here to open up to and allow through the visions and then to put into place and build and create and practice the new ways. You are not here to do this all at once. It is still a process. Take your time. Be patient. Be understanding. Be kind.

But show up. Do your part. Remember your many many lessons of Capricorn. Remember to keep letting go of all of the ways and things and energies that do not serve this new way. Remember why YOU in particular came to this planet. You came because you have a piece of the puzzle to bring through that can only come through YOU. You came because you have gifts for envisioning and creating and building this new way in ways that only YOU can do. This is why you are here. Keep listening. Keep allowing through YOUR wisdom, your knowings, your visions, your gifts, what existence is sharing through YOU. And you will experience beautiful things. We see it. Share and connect with each other. You need each other in this time. The Age of Aquarius is about the collective. It is about connecting and envisioning and working in and for groups and for the good of all. That is your mission. That is the mission of us all. Thank you so much for being here.

The Cosmic Flow Through You

Today on this Solstice day in which Jupiter conjuncts Saturn at 0 degrees Aquarius, I feel the celebratory energy of the potential of this day and of this conjunction. I also know that creating a new world and a new way will continue to have challenges and will take a lot of work on my part, as well as of the people and world around me. I am dedicated and devoted to doing my part.

Today I celebrate this moment and know that mine to do is...

My vision for moving into this Age of Aquarius is….

My part in making this vision happen is….

Right here and right now I commit to….

I came to this planet to….

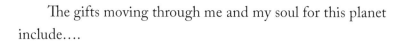

The gifts moving through me and my soul for this planet include….

I am needed right here and right now and I am in exactly the right place at exactly the right time. This feels like….

I am grateful to be alive in this body, right here and right now. I am surrounded by exactly who and what I need to do my part to bring into fruition "mine to do" as we all move into this new time and this new way. I feel surrounding me….

I am held. I am known. I am needed. Right here. Right now. I am loved. I am so fully appreciated. I love all of existence and I am loved right back. So it is. Amen.

TUESDAY, DECEMBER 29, 2020

FULL MOON IN CANCER, 8 degrees, 7:28pm, PST

Getting Centered in You

We invite you to start by taking a deep breath, dropping into your true center, your beautiful and pure soul. And from this place, name what is true for you...

Today, I am feeling...

In this moment, what is present for me is...

Today, I am needing...

Today, mine to do is...

Our Message for You

Today is the last full moon in 2020. It is a full moon in Cancer. This full moon in Cancer adds a sweet, soft ending to this year of intensity, hard work, and incredible transformation.

We want to take this opportunity to hold you, to say good job, to say we know how hard you worked, how much you put into this past year. We want to say how much we appreciate that you went to the deepest parts of yourself, to the most vulnerable and raw parts of yourself - over and over and over again. We want to thank you also for letting go, for letting die the parts of yourself and your world that needed to come crashing down, that were no longer helpful to creating the new way, the new vision coming through you and through those visioning the world with you.

This was likely incredibly difficult at times and also hopefully blissful and happy at other times. This was all great and needed work - for yourself, for your relationships, for your communities, and for the collective as a whole.

We invite you to take this opportunity of the sun shining on the full moon in Cancer to feel into that raw, most vulnerable part of yourself and give yourself some time to feel what you are needing to enter fully into the coming year of 2021 feeling held and met and nurtured and cared for in exactly the ways you need it.

You have endured a lot, gone through a lot, put in a great deal of work, and now it is important to come back to this deep center home in yourself and feel into what you are needing deep down inside too.

So on this day of the last full moon of the year 2020 in the sign of Cancer, I take a deep breath and feel into my most raw, most vulnerable part of myself. What I feel and see and know in this part of myself is….

What the most raw and vulnerable part of me needs right now is….

I am surrounded with love and care and nurturing and can get what I need from inside myself and also by….

I say thank you to the year 2020. As I head toward the energies of 2021 and this new age we are collectively entering, I leave behind….

As I head into 2021, I take with me....

I give gratitude for....

I have so much love moving through and around me....

I give a big hug to myself, to all of existence, and existence hugs me back.

Thank you 2020. And welcome 2021....

ABOUT MARTHA

Martha Alter Hines, MSW, CMT is a channel and a cosmic healer. She has over twenty years of experience as a psychotherapist, clinical social worker, and body worker.

She now assists people to navigate the beautiful and often challenging experience of awakening to their ultimate, cosmic selves and their pure soul truth, soul gifts, and soul lives. She has the ability to see people's actual souls, their energy bodies, past lives, spiritual worlds, and the energy bodies and structures of the Earth and of the cosmos. Martha is in constant communication with a wide range of spiritual energies and existences.

She is the author of the Living the Light series, eight channeled books that are voices of many of these entities. Each book is a different medicine to assist people in their awakening journeys. The first book, Living the One Light, was published in 2018. Gaia Speaks and Cosmos Speaks were published in 2019, and the next five are soon to come.

Martha has two wonderful children and lives in gorgeous Goleta, California. Martha loves the coast of California and feels called to be co-creating with this place for a long time to come.

Connect with Martha at www.livingtheonelight.com and livingtheonelight@gmail.com.

Made in the USA
Columbia, SC
20 February 2020